my MOM is not my MONEY

A TEENAGER'S GUIDE
TO EARNING YOUR OWN MONEY

by
Allie Joy

FOREWORD BY
Mary Morrissey

LifeSOULutions That Work LLC

Disclaimer: While the money-making and other advice in this book is believed to be effective, there is no guarantee that any venture undertaken based on this book will be profitable owing to the general risks involved in any business and specific challenges a reader may face given the nature and location of the venture in question. Nothing associated with this book shall constitute any kind of representation, warranty, promise or guaranty of profitability, earnings, investments, outcomes or successes. A reader's success in obtaining certain results may depend on a number of factors including market conditions and the reader's skill, knowledge, ability, dedication, business savvy and financial situation. Any forward-looking statements associated with this book are simply statements of possibilities, not representations, warranties, promises or guaranties.

This book should not be deemed to offer any professional, personal, mental, psychological, medical, health, financial, accounting, investment, tax, legal or other professional advice. This book does not replace or substitute for the services of trained professionals in any field, including, but not limited to, mental, psychological, medical, health, financial, accounting, investment, tax, legal or other professional fields.

LifeSOULutions That Work, LLC, as well as the author, owner, or publisher of this book and/or or their respective owners, officers, directors, employees, agents, successors or assigns shall not have any liability for any direct, indirect, consequential, special, exemplary, compensatory or other damages, claims, liabilities or losses that may be sustained by the use of the advice in this book and any such liability is hereby expressly disclaimed.

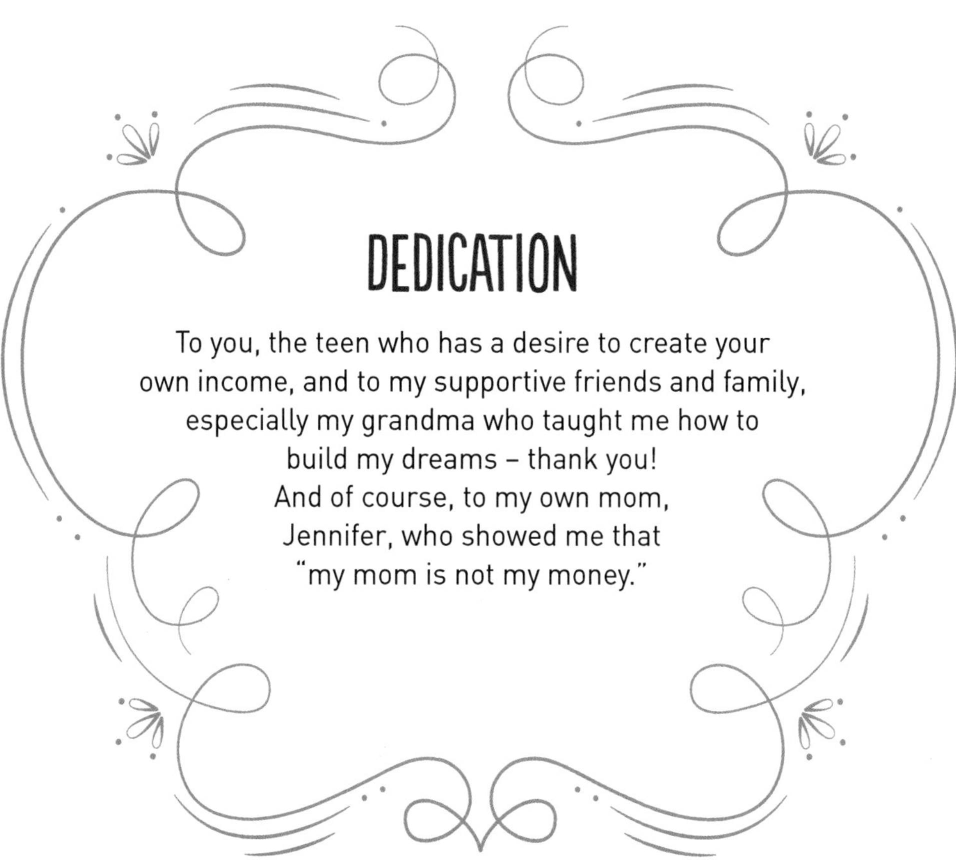

DEDICATION

To you, the teen who has a desire to create your own income, and to my supportive friends and family, especially my grandma who taught me how to build my dreams – thank you!
And of course, to my own mom, Jennifer, who showed me that "my mom is not my money."

About the Author

Allie Joy is a pretty normal teenage girl, believe it or not. She's on the cheer squad, loves to dance, eat food, and enjoys reading books such as "A Fault in Our Stars." She's into music, tumblr and absolutely loves a good Starbucks run.

But a big difference between Allie Joy and most other teenagers is that she doesn't rely solely on her parents for cash, and thinks other kids shouldn't either. She decided to take what she knows and has learned through her successful family, and put it into a book of her own. She also sincerely hopes this book will help you to be a successful moneymaker as well.

Author's Acknowledgments

First, I would like to thank my Grandma for letting me come to *DreamBuilder LIVE*, where I first learned how to sell my products at the young age of ten. I would also like to thank my dad, for explaining to me the structure of writing a book, and sitting me down to write the first 10 pages (that have now become this book), and a huge "thank you" goes to my mom for supporting me every step of the way. Thanks also to my younger brothers, Joel and Joaquin, for letting me practice my salesmanship skills on them by selling them my old books and toys. Thank you to all my extended family, my aunts, uncles, and cousins, for lending ideas, stories, and your gracious support. Another thanks goes out to all the young adults who lent their great moneymaking stories. I am also very grateful to Cathy Lynn for lending her writing expertise and to Judi Paliungas and her team at Palimor Studios for creating a beautifully designed cover and book. And also thanks to Jim Paliungas for the amazing photography. Lastly, I'd like to say thank you to all of my friends for their love and support.

FOREWORD

by Mary Morrissey

In 2006, Allie Joy, the author of this book, and I were having breakfast together.

Allie was seven years old and the waitress had given her four crayons and a menu that had children's games on the back side of it.

I noticed Allie beginning to do the maze puzzle game. While she did this, I perused the menu to decide what I would order, and when I glanced up about 15 seconds later, Allie had her hands in the air and said, "Look, Ama (her name for me), I am done!"

I was surprised she had finished so quickly and asked, "Allie, how did you accomplish your goal so fast?" This little seven-year-old looked up and smiled at me and said, "Oh it's easy. You just start at the place you want to end up and work backwards and it's SO much faster!"

I was astonished and amazed. I had spent years of study to discover the power of accelerating the goal-achieving process through reverse engineering and here this amazing seven-year-old had figured it out for herself.

Allie Joy is my first-born granddaughter.

I have been both a student and teacher of success principles for over 40 years. Allie started attending my seminars when she was 10 years old and has been applying all she intuitively knew and all she has learned about how successful people think and how they treat each moment and opportunity.

Over the years that have transpired, I have been privileged to witness Allie Joy, time and time again, begin with her goal in mind and achieve results quicker and easier than most people ever expect.

I am proud of Allie's willingness to study and test these principles for herself. I have had so much fun seeing her create her own freedom to go and do and give what she wanted and I am grateful for her decision to want to pass on what she has learned to you. It's simply easier to get where you want to go when you have a map!

The book you are about to read is the map and it has REAL POWER in it. The principles and tools included have been "road tested" and work.

But even the most powerful car cannot do anything if left in the driveway. Take these ideas in Allie's book "out for a spin" and see your results accelerate.

This book is all about the freedom for you to do and have and give what you would love – and now, you hold these secrets in your hands!

Welcome to "My Mom Is Not My Money" and the freedom and fun that comes when you know you can create your own results.

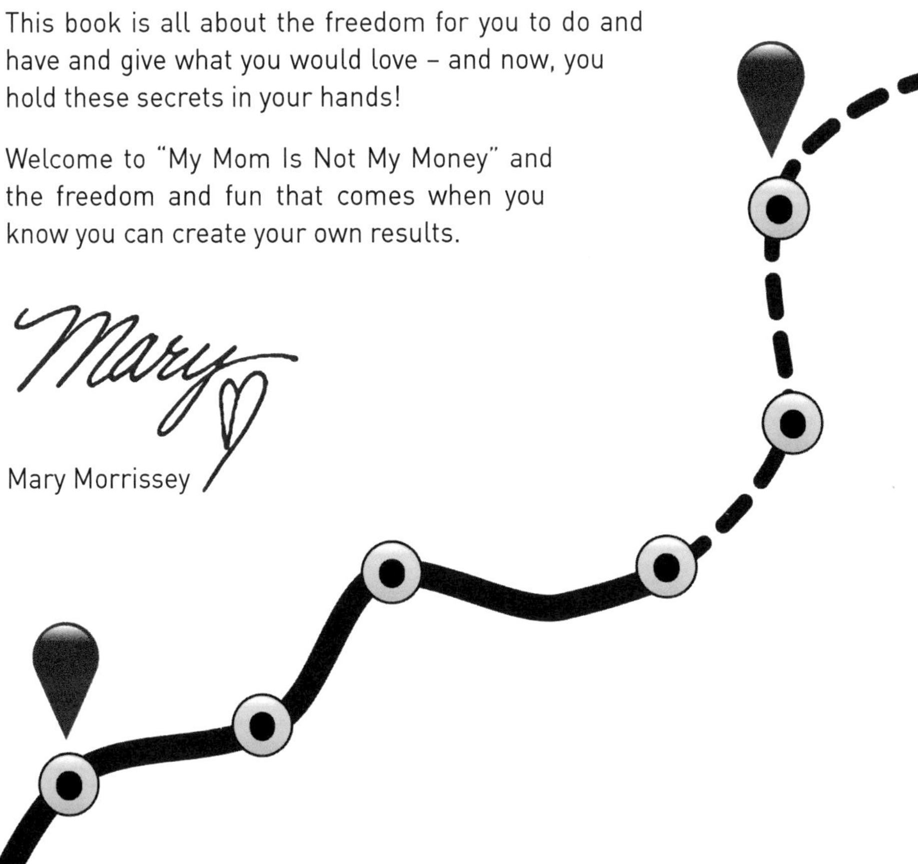

Mary Morrissey

TABLE OF CONTENTS

"Money is only a tool. It will take you wherever you wish, but it will not replace you as the driver."

—Ayn Rand

INTRODUCTION

I'm gonna guess you are approaching this book in one of three ways. 1) You haven't bought it yet and you're checking it out either for yourself or someone you know. 2) You've already bought the book or someone gave it to you because you really want your own cash (which, by the way, is pretty awesome). 3) Your parents or someone else is making you read this and you are rolling your eyes dreading the next few pages.

No matter how you got here, just know that you are in the right place. Really, what are the chances that this book is in your hands? It's packed with ideas for you to create your own money magic and it's buzzing with energy. So congrats...you are in for a treat.

If you are the one who is rolling your eyes, all I ask is that you cage up any negative thoughts roaming around in your mind, because that's the kind of attitude that will limit your success. I am going to ask you to have an open mind and give this book a chance. If you do, I can promise you will be glad you did and once you have read these pages, you will be equipped with some new powerful tools that can literally change your life...both financially and otherwise.

Who Is Allie Joy?

So you are probably wondering, who is this teenager? What does she know about making money, and why should I listen to her? Well, my name is Allie, and ever since I was little, like most of us, I relied on my parents for cash, lunch money, clothing money, and any other extra spending bucks.

Until the time I asked my mom for $40 to go to the mall and she said no. I was like, "Why not? I don't have any other money!" This wasn't the first time I'd ever asked for money. Plenty of times I had asked for money, then crossed my fingers hoping and praying to the magic wallet genie that she would say "yes." But this time she came back with a "no" and an invitation.

My mom said, "Well, I could either give you the money, or I could help you learn how to earn it yourself." She went on to say, "Allie, I want you to know I am not the only source of money you can tap into. Actually, I would love to show you how you have the ability to tap into the power of your imagination anytime you want to generate money-making ideas. Which would you prefer? That I give you the money, or I teach you how to make your own money?"

At first I was like, "Give me the money" of course, but a light went off in my head at the thought of making my own money! That was when it all kind of clicked for me and I decided to give it a try.

INTRODUCTION

How I Made My First Money

My mom helped me to tap into my imagination by making a list of all the things I could sell or "done for you" services I could offer. I was 10 at the time, and looked at what I loved to do, and how I could somehow fill a need by doing what I enjoyed doing. I also looked for things that were within my reach.

The immediate need I saw came from watching my mom sell her own products at my grandma Mary Morrissey's personal development conference called DreamBuilder LIVE. My mom had a table at the back of the room where she would sell her stuff, and she needed an extra set of hands. So, I made a deal with my mom. I offered to help her sell her things, and at the same time, I would be allowed to sell my own things as well.

She liked the idea, so I thought about how jewelry and accessories would be fun. Then my mom told me about the fashion mart where I could buy anything and everything fashion-related in bulk and at a low cost.

I was like...yeah, that could be fun! When we got there, the fashion mart was like this huge maze, and we were on a hunt searching for the right treasures. After awhile, I finally found what I wanted to buy. Then we returned home, and my mom and I packaged the jewelry nicely and priced each item for sale. I made sure that I sold the jewelry for a price that allowed me to pay back my Mom for the cost of the jewelry, and also make a profit on top for myself.

At the conference, we had a full table to display our products. My mom taught me how to welcome people to the table and spark up a conversation. Not everyone I spoke to bought something, but my mom had told me that, "Sales is a numbers game." If you offer your product to enough people, and there's good value in what you have, someone will eventually buy it. And they did!

I learned a lot about how to sell, run a cash box, add up prices, talk to customers, and believe it or not, it was really fun. It was kind of like running a mini store. And at the end of the day, I sold 70% of what I had to sell. It was not as easy as I first thought and it ended up being a long day and a lot of hard work. But it was certainly worth it because after I paid my Mom back, I had made 300 bucks!

The best part was seeing that money in my wallet and knowing I had earned every single penny of it...and that I had the freedom to spend it on what I really wanted to buy. Plus, my parents were really proud of me. I had successfully stepped out of my comfort zone and I overcame being a bit shy.

And this was just the beginning of many money-making ventures to come. I then started exploring other ways to use my gifts and talents to make a profit by looking for needs and filling them the best I could.

For example, later on, my Grandma needed help organizing her house and office. I could certainly do that! One thing led to another and I also organized her suitcase, then her jewelry, cupboards, and even wrapped all of her Christmas presents (except for mine of course). I also expanded outside my family and did some babysitting jobs and tutoring for a fee. These were all things I could easily do on my own, and talents that I was able to turn into money simply by seeing and filling the needs around me and finding ways to serve people.

What's In This for You?

As I started to earn my own income, you'd hear many adults always telling me how lucky I was to have the knowledge of how to do it. Especially at the DreamBuilder LIVE events, everyone would always come up to me and tell me how special it was to have an amazing family. They'd also say how they wished they had been exposed to this knowledge and learned these tools when they were my age.

This brought something to my attention. I saw that all of my friends were still relying on their families as the one and only source of money. As more and more people told me, "I wish I had learned how to make my own cash when I was a kid," and, "I would like my kids to learn how to make their own cash too," I began to think...

And that is when I came up with the idea for this book. I thought, "How can I help all kids get this information and have the power to earn their own income?"

But in order to write this book, I needed money to create it. So I got this idea to pre-sell the book and made $600.00 in advance. One thing led to another while I took the steps I could with what I had, and now you have this book in your hands (or maybe on your smart phone or tablet). And if you keep reading to see how easy it really is to make your own money, soon you'll also have your own cash to buy what you want without asking anyone but yourself for money.

Get ready. By learning and applying the tools in this book, together we can create a new generation of teens who are not just hypnotized by social media, but are empowered and confident to go out into the world and make their own spending money, whenever we want!

HOW THIS BOOK IS ORGANIZED

This book is organized into five parts, which cover everything from coming up with "money-making ideas" to how to use money wisely. I've even come up with an easy way to remember the five steps of making money by using an acronym D.R.E.A.M. The D is for ***Discover***, R for ***Reach Out***, E for ***Endeavor***, A for ***Achieve***, and of last but not least, M is for ***Manage***.

"D" ...is for Discover

This is where you will "discover" your dream and find out what you already love, what you are good at, and how you can turn your passion and interests into money making ideas. Don't worry if you think you have no ideas yet, I've collected a bunch of cool ones that will help spark your imagination.

"R" ...is for Reach Out

One of the primary tools in generating money is to allow your family, friends, and maybe teachers or someone you know, to help you. This is where you "reach out" and develop relationships with those who can help. You might need to find someone to bounce ideas off of, teach you a skill, borrow something from, loan you some seed money, or other resources in order to help you succeed.

"E" ...is for Endeavor

When you "endeavor" to reach your dream, sometimes you need to start taking action even before you feel ready and at some point, you will need to face your fears. The word endeavor means to "try hard to do or achieve something." This is where you start with what you already have, and take action in the direction of your dreams... one step at a time.

"A" ...is for Achieve

At this stage, if you follow the steps I lay out here in this book, you will begin to see results and earn some money. This is the "achieve" part and the fun part. But you will also most likely see some failure. The trick is that when you do fail, do not give up. You will need to learn how to dust yourself off, keep moving forward, and how to use the power of persistence to your advantage.

"M" ...is for Manage

Money, money, money! Soon enough you will be able to see how, through the power of your imagination, it's easier to make money than you might think. And once you start making it, you will be able to "manage" those little green slips. You might even want to read this chapter first. So you can start with the end in mind and prepare the field for what's coming. You can have a plan for what to do with your money once you have earned it. You can then make better action items, and be able to gain control of your own money system.

DREAM

Whichever way you choose, either beginning with the end in mind or starting with the first chapter on using your imagination... just do it and get started! I promise, you will be glad you did.

Part I

DISCOVER

THE ART OF IMAGINATION

"There are two kinds of dreams. There are dreams that we have while asleep and dreams that we have while we are awake. What is the connection between the two types? Both kinds of dreams are about the yearnings that are held deep inside us. Some of these desires are so secret that we dare not share them even with our closest friends. Those of us that dare to put our dreams down on paper are showing the courage and faith that they will come true."

– Author Unknown

THE ART OF IMAGINATION

In This Chapter

- ✔ Using our imaginations and seeing the possibilities
- ✔ Exploring why you want to make money and testing your ideas
- ✔ Taking a look towards the future and creating your vision

"LIFE IS SIMPLY SEEKING YOUR AWARENESS AND DIRECTION THROUGH INTELLIGENT USE OF THE POWER OF YOUR THOUGHT, FOR THE GOOD YOU DESIRE TO EXPERIENCE AND GIVE."

— MARY MORRISSEY

Ever watch the movie *Inception*? It really made you think, didn't it? Kinda like what's real and what's not. So this is where I'd like to begin this book, by exploring our creative side by using our imaginations.

Okay, so are you ready? Here we go. Let's start by taking a look at what we *really* love, what we are already good at, and take these ideas and turn them into some cash by thinking outside the box.

In this first chapter, we'll dive into discovering your why and connecting to your dream. We will also do a Six-Step Test to make sure your dream is really right for you.

We'll then look at what it takes to create a solid money-making "blueprint" and some other fun stuff that will begin to give you a roadmap towards your very own treasure chest of money.

DISCOVER YOUR DREAM

It can be almost overwhelming, but there are so many different money-making possibilities out there to try — and I don't just mean hard, crummy or boring physical laboring work. Sure, you can work at a fast food place, if that is what you enjoy, but the simplest ideas and hobbies can also be a way to make you some cash.

DREAM

And I'm talking about serious $$.

Check this out. I heard of this 14-year-old kid whose grandma taught him to make jam. He started selling this jam around his neighborhood. Then in only two years, he'd sold his jam into 184 store locations, and now his jam is sold in most of the major stores.

Just do the math on that!

HINT: It's over 1 million dollars.

Okay, I get it and so do you. But what the heck? We are talking about jam, not some major blockbuster movie, but a simple fruit spread. Amazing!

There's this other kid, who at age 9, started selling invitation cards, and at 11, he had raised enough money to form his own company. Then by age 15, he was receiving big residual checks every month, enough to pay for a house, a car, or college, or whatever...!

How cool is that? Are you starting to see how even the simplest of ideas can be turned into fast cash? And WHO said that teens can't make big money?

I, for one, know we can. I've done it for myself.

So, let's begin. What can you dream up and create? And I'm beginning to feel like it's gonna be just great! Nothing you could decide to do is either too small or too big... you just need to look deep down in your heart and dig, dig dig.

Oh well... I tried to rhyme, but you get the point! Ha-ha.

THINK OUTSIDE THE BOX

Let Your Imagination Run Wild

"I WANT TO SHOW THAT THE POSSIBILITIES ARE ENDLESS. THAT'S MY GOAL – TO NOT ONLY DO IT FOR MYSELF, BUT TO SHOW THAT I CAN DO WHATEVER I PUT MY MIND TO."

— NICKI MINAJ

Imagine going to the mall and being able to pick out anything you wanted without flinching at the price tag. NO, I mean REALLY, imagine going to the mall, or the Internet, or anywhere you would love to shop, and being able to just look and decide what YOU would really love to have (do or give).

Yet, we are never really *taught* this way of thinking. Almost everyone has been taught to believe they have to seek a basic human life. We just go to school, graduate, get into a good college, pick a career, meet this great guy or girl, fall in love, get married, get a job, and then maybe down the road, you can maybe buy a house and have financial freedom (even though you are still gonna have to deal with taxes).

How about when you're in high school and everyone's telling you to get a summer job, at like a frozen yogurt place. You do that. Go ahead. That's one option. Work hours and hours, weeks upon weeks to save up every penny you can to get enough for your own car, and probably a used one at that!

So Here's Your First Test

If I present the possibility of making enough money to buy your own car right now, a custom-made, brand-new ride, what would you say? Most people would likely roll their eyes and say, "I wish."

Case in point, I was talking to one of my closest friends about what kind of car we wanted to have and I said "Yeah, I would like to custom design my own car. Have the outside like a pearl white and inside a cream color" or whatever, just throwing spaghetti on the wall (a term I use when I'm just throwing ideas out there).

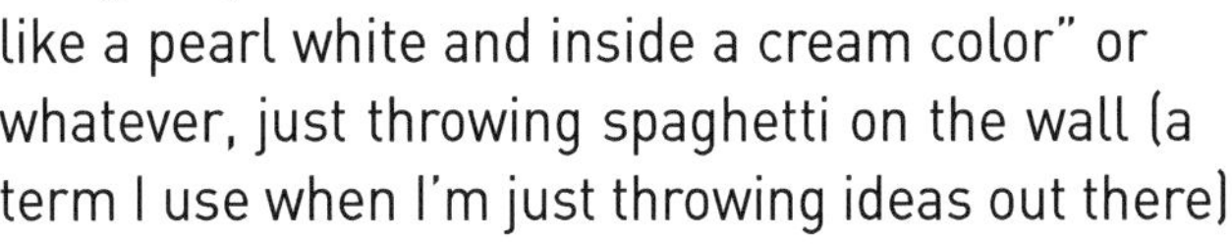

When she heard me say *custom design*, she laughed and was like, "Yeah, I am barely saving up for a used car, let alone a custom-made one. Wow, that would be like SO expensive!" I was "Yeah. okay..." but we didn't get to continue because our teacher caught us talking!

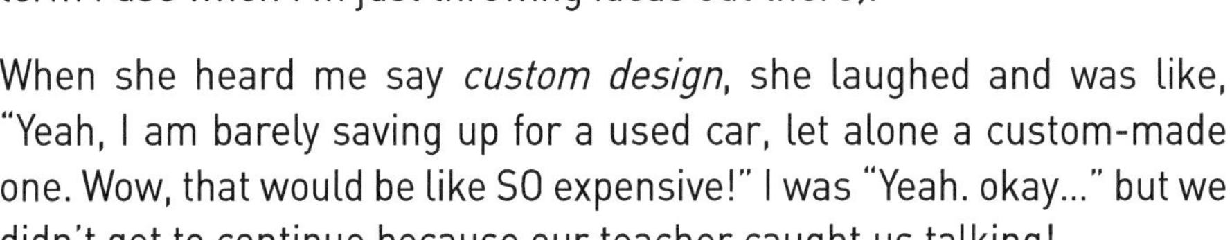

But you get the point. Honestly, a car is just one of the many possibilities that are out there to explore.

And my friend is a perfect example of what most of us were taught to believe growing up, and what most of our parents were taught, and grandparents too. We have all pretty much been told to first *have* the money, or see "how" to do it, before going after our dreams.

Hold on. I'm here to tell you that this is a backwards way of thinking. If Walt Disney had waited until he knew *how* and waited until he *saved up* all the money, Disneyland wouldn't even exist!!!

Get the Ball Rolling

To get the ball rolling with ideas of your own, let me give you twelve quick and really easy ways you can get into the game of making some extra money. None of these may earn you enough cash to get your own custom made car, but they definitely will get you started in the right direction:

- ✔ Organize a family (or neighborhood) garage sale
- ✔ Wash cars or babysit kids
- ✔ Lemonade or cookie/cupcake stand
- ✔ Sell snacks at your local soccer field at half-time
- ✔ Dog walking or pet sitting in the neighborhood
- ✔ Cleaning or organizing for family members
- ✔ Shoveling snow or raking leaves
- ✔ Tutoring or music/singing lessons
- ✔ Sports coaching or skateboard lessons
- ✔ Offer to do extra chores for extra cash
- ✔ Sell used items on eBay (like American Girl dolls or X-Box games, etc.)

There are many other ways, and the best part is going to be for you to tap into your own creative imagination to think of ideas and get started putting some cash in your wallet. This will be a big magnet for more ideas and further actions you can take.

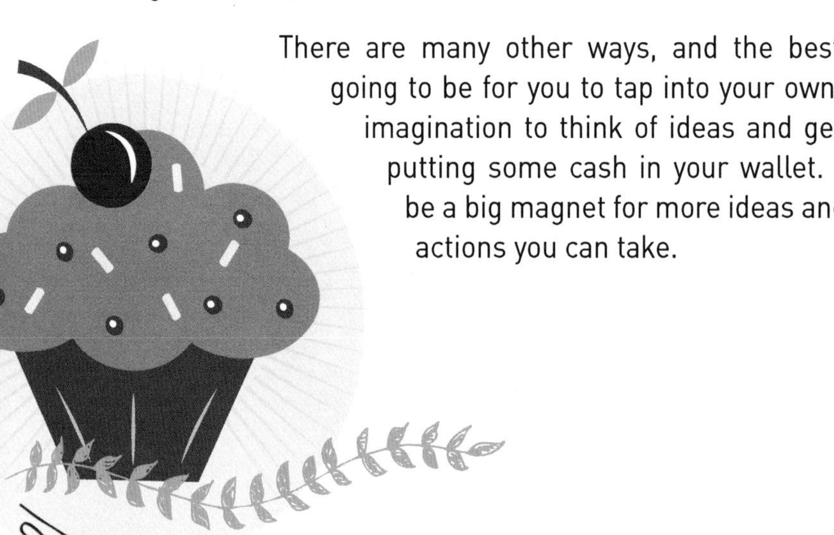

EXPLORING THE POSSIBILITIES

Hooking the Great Ideas

"ONE IDEA LEADS TO ANOTHER, LIKE BUBBLES...THE TRICK IS TO CATCH THEM BEFORE THEY DISAPPEAR."
— UNKNOWN

As I mentioned at the beginning of this chapter, my first piece of advice for you is to focus on what you love, and do what you enjoy doing.

Would you rather do tutoring or teaching as a job, or play with little kids and get paid for it? Most any idea can be turned into cash. So why not do something you have fun doing? It could be sports, dance, cooking, drawing, playing video games, or even gardening.

Each one of those can actually earn you the big bucks.

These ideas and others have lots of opportunities locked up and hidden within them. You just have to find the key to unlock their potential. And that key is to make sure you have a burning desire for what the money will bring to you (or someone else).

Don't trade your time for something you don't love. Even if you don't want to develop every idea into a business. Really, any idea can be expanded on and taken to wherever you want it to go. No limits here.

Your money making idea can run a mile or a marathon – be big or small. It is all up to you to give it the right amount of fuel and support to glide it through the finish line. Which, of course in this case, is the freedom of money in your wallet to do, have, and give what matters to you most.

Things That You Are Good At and That Are Fun

It's time to get started by coming up with *your* list of ideas. Even though we are going to talk more in depth about setting goals a little bit later, for now let's just pick one to give you something tangible to work with.

Pick a short term goal, like making a quick $40 for a new pair of jeans or a dress, or a long term goal, like saving up for a new bike or a new car.

So, what's your goal? Is it a short term goal, or a long term goal? Write it down.

Here's an example:

- ✔ a new pair of $40 jeans by next Saturday night
- ✔ a new Mustang convertible by my 17th birthday

Now that you have something in mind, let's come up with ideas that could support that desire. Okay, so it's time for you to grab a notebook or piece of paper.

And no cheating...it must be a regular sized sheet!

Go ahead, and write down all the things you *love* to do and what you are *good* at (and can do on your own).

For example, here are a few of mine:

- ✔ I have little brothers and I am good with kids
- ✔ I speak fluent Spanish
- ✔ I am creative and like to draw and paint
- ✔ I am a good writer (poetry, lyrics, stories, etc.)
- ✔ I love animals
- ✔ I like to bake

Okay, so those were just some ideas right off the top of my head. Now, I want you to fill out an entire page with your own ideas and leave some space in between each of them. Remember, what you *love* and what you are *good* at. Go, do this NOW.

Once you have written down a half dozen ideas or so that come to mind, add underneath each one, some money-making activities that go along with each idea, especially things you are really good at doing.

What we are looking to discover here is how each of the things you put down on this list could generate some cash to help you get the money you want.

Your ideas don't have to be perfect. They can even include weird stuff like 'jam maker' or good with a cell phone, or whatever. No rules, except you need to write down *at least 20 ideas or more.*

Notice what happens after about idea #10.

Muck Comes Up First

I'm going to tell you a secret. My grandma says, when you're pumping water from a well, the first thing that comes up is dirty mucky stuff. But then you create a vacuum that literally "sucks" the crystal clear water from deep within the earth right up through the pipe and into your own container.

So when trying to come up with ideas that can make some money, my advice again is to look towards what you love doing most to create this vacuum effect, then start pumping out the ideas until you receive clarity.

Don't worry about those mucky water ideas and "how" you are going to do these things. Forget that for now... and just start writing down all the ideas. Let 'em flow. Keep writing them down until you can't think of any more, then pause for awhile and allow a few more to come flowing into your head. Write these down too.

The next step is to take your dreams and interests and allow your imagination to take those ideas and connect the dots. Out of all the ideas you've come up with, pick at least two or three ideas to make money.

For example, here are my personal ideas:

I have little brothers and I am good with kids:

- ✔ I can babysit
- ✔ I can tutor
- ✔ I can teach kids Spanish

I am creative:

- ✔ I can sell art
- ✔ I can sell poems
- ✔ I can teach kids how to make fun crafts
- ✔ I can make and sell hand-designed cupcakes in my neighborhood

I love animals:

- ✔ I can start a dog walking business
- ✔ I can offer pet sitting
- ✔ I can make custom pet accessories

Now that you're getting my point, write down on your own piece of paper your ideas and add all the creative ways you can think of that you can make money with each of the gifts and talents you already have.

TIP: *From now on, always keep a journal and pencil with you, or just use your notes app on your smart phone or tablet.*

Crystal Clarity

It's pretty funny how this process works. After putting down about 10 ideas or so, our mind tends to get out of the way (or gets emptied out)... and that's when new ideas just start showing up out of nowhere. They begin to flow through as if by magic or something.

And don't worry if some look a bit crazy or weird. At the end of the day, these might end up being the best ones yet. So, have you got your list finished yet?

Woo hoo! Give yourself a BIG pat on the back!! Say to yourself, "I'm on my way to the bank!"

WARNING: Do not go on to the next part of this book *until* you've actually done the idea pumping list above.

I can show you how to make your own money, but not if you don't do your part. No one can think up your own ideas but YOU. So take a moment and do it now!

Okay, so what happens next?

Well, let's take a peek at *why* the money is important to you...just to give it some anchoring strength.

Don't worry, we'll get back to our idea list in just a second (when we dive into the energy factor). But for now here's a HINT: It has to do with *electricity*.

DETERMINE YOUR WHY

Here's a really good question to ask yourself, and the perfect time to ask it. "WHY do you want to make some extra money?" Do you want to buy yourself (or another person) something specific?

An example might be; a new pair of jeans, an Xbox, an iPad, go to a great concert, etc. Or is your dream to earn money so you can take dance classes or music lessons? Maybe you'd like to buy your Mom a nice Christmas gift, or raise money for your local animal shelter, church...you name it. So what do you want?

It's always good to have something tangible in mind.

While doing my online research, I found quite a few kids and teens who have done some pretty amazing things. They've accomplished huge goals and dreams and raised all types of money for a good cause. Why?

Because they had a big "why!"

A great example of this is Christy Levine, who at age 15 discovered her dream was to help kids with disabilities. She then went about raising $5,000 for BAORP (Bay Area Outreach and Recreation Program) which serves youth with physical disabilities.

Amazing!! She's 15 and gave away $5,000?? Wow, who does that? Well, Christy Levine does and here's the deal. You, too, can do whatever you set your mind to when you learn a few of the powerful things I'll be showing you here within this book.

I think it's so cool that you're reading this book. Who knows what great things you'll be inspired to do too!

CONNECTING TO THE IDEAS

Your Inner Genius

"THE BIGGEST ADVENTURE YOU CAN TAKE IS TO LIVE THE LIFE OF YOUR DREAMS."

—OPRAH WINFREY

Do yourself a favor and go back to take a look at your list. It's time to add the things you'd like to buy (or give to someone, or other ways to make a difference) if you had all of your own money. Remember to keep in mind your "why" ideas from above.

We are doing this so that you can really connect to these ideas at your core and anchor them to you.

Again, write down all the ideas that come to you, even the bad ones...I mean it! Remember, what you need to do is to NOT edit your ideas. When they first show up, just write them down as they come to you.

Shy Introductions

You may have already noticed this, but by doing these idea generating lists, your inner genius is becoming less shy and finally introducing itself. Literally, this happens just by writing down everything that pops into your mind. Some call it daydreaming, but my Grandma Mary Morrissey, who is a speaker, author, consultant, and the entire family calls it "dream building" (in fact, we are truly a bloodline of "dream builders").

It's really cool stuff and I can teach you what they've taught me. This whole process of dreaming big, and thinking outside the box and writing everything down are great tools to work with. And, one really important point to remember is when you write down all the ideas that come to you, you are actually creating a vacuum for your genius.

Yes, you actually have access to genius ideas...similar to Einstein! It's just that most of us teens keep our minds so busy with games, TV, and gadgets, that we don't take the time to allow these ideas to show up! Think about this for a minute. This is gonna get a little scientific, but stick with me here. The wind doesn't blow, the wind sucks. Just like with a low-pressure front, it pulls the air towards itself and creates this vacuum effect.

You see, we call it the wind blowing, but literally it's air rushing past us to a low-pressure zone. It's not a pushing, but a pulling effect and quite literally, this is a law of nature. You can't see this at work, but it's the same thing as getting great ideas. This is what great thinkers and inventors like Einstein and Thomas Edison accessed. And we all know what kinds of ideas they came up with. Cool, huh?

How do you know a great idea, or even genius idea, from a not so great one? Well it has to do with electricity. Now, remember this term, because I'm going to be saying this a lot, since it's very important.

Take a look at electric energy... how you use this power will either electrocute you or light up your room. And, knowing you have control over how you use this power is also pretty cool to think about.

Now back to whether your idea is a great one or a not so great one. We'll test them. But, just be sure that along the way you don't say "No, that's a bad idea," and discount it before writing it down. Put everything that shows up in your mind down on your list and keep fishing for more ideas.

This will make sure you have a big bucket full, and you can then choose which ones will be the keepers and which ones eventually need to be thrown back!

Focus On the Juice

When looking at your list of ideas, it's really important to ask yourself, "What do I really love to do?" What do I want to buy? And what do I want to give to someone else, or what are other ways to make a difference if I had all the $$ in the world?

By doing this, you filter out those pesky distractions and doubts, those things that aren't really aligned with who you are really meant to be.

For example, let's say I love to paint. Not sure how that can make me rich just yet, but I'm gonna explore the possibilities by writing down them down anyway:

- ✔ I love painting
- ✔ I love the rich colors and texture of paint
- ✔ I love creating something new and original
- ✔ I love expressing my passion for beautiful art
- ✔ I love seeing amazing beautiful things...

Got the idea? Now it's time for you to write these things down and develop your own list.

Having fun? Great!

Expand Your Horizons

Whatever you do, don't fall into the trap of thinking only about what you feel is possible. Always go for what you want. Elevate your thinking and expand the possibilities.

FOR EXAMPLE: "If I could do anything and knew I couldn't fail, this is what I'd love to do..."

- ✔ paint in my free time
- ✔ paint for my friends and their families
- ✔ paint professionally

- ✔ have my paintings hang in the Getty Museum
- ✔ have my artwork change the world...

When you do this... the world literally opens up. The possibilities expand, and funny thing is, the impossible more times than not, becomes *possible*!

Play with this. Creating is fun. So keep it that way! From here we'll move into the phase of re-examining our ideas. This is where we find out which of our ideas is right for us, and which are the ones to focus on.

TESTING YOUR IDEAS

Seeing What Is Right for You

"YOU WERE BORN TO BE SOMEBODY, MAYBE A VET, MAYBE A HERO, MAYBE A CAREGIVER. WHATEVER IT IS YOU WERE BORN TO BE SOMETHING SPECIAL AND IF YOU BELIEVE...YOU CAN ACHIEVE."
– JUSTIN BIEBER

At this point, you've tossed around some big ideas, dreams, and money-making concepts that might seem like great possibilities to act upon. And of course, they all sound pretty exciting to you, because they're based on what you love and are good at. Cool.

Well, now's the time to test them out and see if they are actually perfect for you. It makes sense to see if your ideas are worthy of your time and energy, right?

And, shouldn't we make sure they are in alignment with your core values and purpose? Ok, well you may or may not know what your "purpose" is, that's a pretty deep word, but maybe we should double check, just to be certain these ideas really make you feel alive and excited to try out.

SPECIAL NOTE: In a minute, you're also going to measure which ones are "buzzing with energy" and put a big star next to them. But, just hang tight for now...

This is really huge, because once you begin moving forward on your idea, you want to make sure it has enough energy to motivate you to go the distance with it and see it through to the end.

And there are certain "tests" your ideas must pass.

Okay, this is gonna be fun. Now, it's your opportunity to be the one giving the test instead of being in school and just having to take them all the time. Lol.

Nice, don't you think?

It All Comes Back to Your Why

Why? Because this is where the rubber meets the road. It's the main thing you can always fall back on when you find a few bumps along the way.

The "why" is pretty much the most important thing about your idea. You must test your ideas for the why.

Spend some time really diving into "why" you want whatever it is that you want. Clearly define everything that motivates you to do what you are going to do.

For example, the reason I want to get a car is:

- ✔ to have more freedom to go where I want to go
- ✔ to not have to depend on others

The "why's" like this are so important to put into your overall plans and goal-setting. This is kinda like putting gas in the car or fire under a kettle.

SPECIAL NOTE: More on goal-setting and mapping out a plan in another chapter. But just know, I always like to add my "why" to each and every goal that I set for myself, just as a reminder of the bigger picture that drives my passions forward.

The Five-Step Test

Now that you have some money-making ideas, the next step is to determine whether those ideas are really right for you.

In other words, not whether you're worthy of the idea, but rather, whether the idea is worthy of YOU. My Grandma taught me this: your life is a gift and it's unrepeatable. She showed me this five-step test for determining which ideas to take action on.

Let's see if your ideas hold up to these five questions:

1) Does the idea make me feel alive?
2) Does the idea fit in with my core values?
3) Is it going to require me to stretch a little?
4) Do I need help from others to accomplish this?
5) Is there some good in my idea for others?

Testing your ideas with the above questions supports you in following only those ideas that will ultimately help you grow into becoming a better person. You see, growing is stretching as opposed to staying in your comfort zone, which basically just holds you back.

By moving forward on our ideas and taking small steps to make them happen, we can accomplish more than we once thought possible. How's that for a little confidence booster!

So what's up next? Time to practice "seeing" the future, and imagining your dream coming true. Isn't this exciting? Can you sense the momentum building yet? It's as if I can actually feel your ideas coming to life already...and I'm excited for you!

the Five-Step test

DESIGN THE VISION

What's up with visions and what does this mean? It's like holding a crystal ball and seeing your future success in advance. That's an important step in building a life you love. And once you've written out a clear picture about your vision, you'll then move towards the next step, which is making "committed" steps to achieve those goals.

Again, more details later, 'cause I'm getting ahead of myself. So, let's first dive back into dreaming up an amazing vision for your money-making ideas.

FOLLOW THE ELECTRICITY

Buzzing With Energy

"ENERGY FLOWS WHERE YOUR ATTENTION GOES. PUT YOUR ATTENTION ON THOSE THINGS YOU WANT TO GROW."

– MARY MORRISSEY

Let's work with your list of ideas a bit. Make sure you have a full page of ideas before you move on to this next step. Remember when I hinted that it had something to do with electricity? Well, look over your list of those 20+ things you are good at or enjoy doing.

Run through your list, and find the ideas that seem to have the most electrical charge to them. These are the things that light you up with energy and make you feel more alive.

So, which of those ideas are buzzing with an electric current of energy? Charged up ideas are going to be easier to commit to and see through to the finish line.

Q: How do you know which ones are more electric?

Well, that's easy. Which ones sound the most fun or exciting to you? Which ideas would you still be willing to pursue even after school and homework?

It's as simple as that. These are the ideas that have electricity in them. Highlight, put a star next to, or a big fat circle around them. These are your favorites.

Yay! We are really getting somewhere with this. You now have your list of gifts, talents, hobbies, and have highlighted or put a star next to your favorite ones that have a bit of spark and energy in them.

Before we move on, pick your top one or two ideas from your list of favorites, and make a note of that for later. Great! And now there's only a few more things to do before we begin to turn these ideas into making you some cash.

Your Money-Making Blueprint

I gotta say, one of my big dreams is for this book to provide the tools that become the steps and ladder for you to reach out and grab onto your own success!

And part of that process is what's up next. We get to look into the future and begin molding it for ourselves. Again, it's like looking at our success in advance.

In other words, we "see the future" by creating a blueprint for our ideas. A blueprint is not just a dream of what you wish for in your head...a blueprint is a crystal clear description about your ideas written out like a story (and like I said before, in real time).

It's creating a virtual life vision for your dream. This is a crucial first step in building the structure for your money to show up. Like when you build a house. It's not enough to just have a picture in your mind, you need to design a blueprint for your house on paper.

Script Your Own Story

We've now come to the part of the process where it's time to write your very own personal vision. Once you have mastered this blueprinting tool, it can be used in every area of your life. Again, pretty cool.

Take out another piece of paper (or better yet a journal or notebook). And, before you begin writing, start to imagine in your mind already reaching your goals.

Pulling from those top picks on your ideas list, see in your mind what it'd be like once you've made all the money you want within the time frame you set.

What does it look like when you have already bought the things you wanted to buy, gave the gifts you wanted to give, or made the "difference" with the money you already made?

Next, begin writing down these "storyline" details you have already seen in your imagination. Write it in a future time frame, as if it's already happened. Be as descriptive as you can and put lots of feeling words in it. Pretty much just like a good movie or a great book.

Bring it to life with something like this: *"I am so happy and grateful now that my business is up and running and earning me enough in profits to pay for my own car..."*

Being Courageous

Now don't hold back. This is the time to let yourself go on an adventure. Dream a little (or a LOT) and imagine living out the ideas you have seen in your mind. It's like having that crystal ball in your hands, showing your future the way you want to see it unfold.

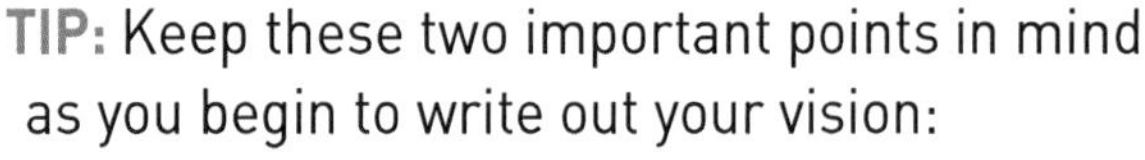

TIP: Keep these two important points in mind as you begin to write out your vision:

1. Why Your Idea Exists

What it's going to do and how it will help other people. For example, if you love animals and your idea is to create a dog walking business, then include something like this:

"I love owning a dog-walking business that helps people have more time and freedom while I am providing a loving and nurturing experience for their dog."

2. What It Feels Like

You also want to *feel* what it will feel like once your ideas have come into existence. You should paint a very vivid and descriptive picture. Something like this:

"It's so cool meeting new dog owners and seeing their eyes light up when I tell them about my business. They love watching me take their dog out for a walk knowing that their dog loves spending time with me."

So tell me, how does this feel? Are you getting a little loose and enjoying the process so far? Good for you!

POWER OF INTENTION

Thoughts Become Things

"I LEARNED A LONG TIME AGO THAT IF I REALLY WANTED TO BRING MY IDEAS TO LIFE, I NEEDED TO WRITE DOWN MY INTENTIONS. WHEN YOU PUT PEN TO PAPER, THERE IS LITTLE CHOICE BUT TO GET SPECIFIC."
– MARY MORRISSEY

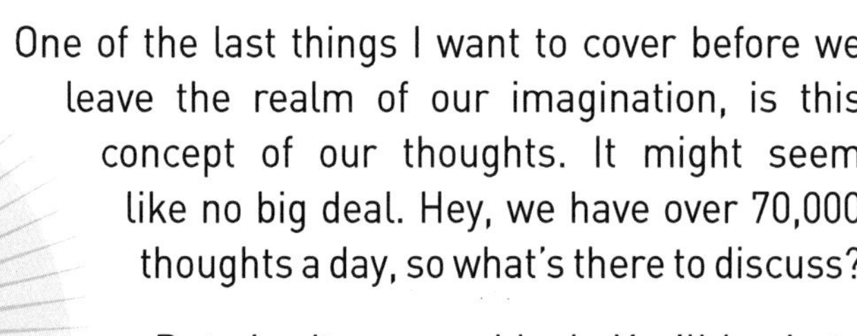

One of the last things I want to cover before we leave the realm of our imagination, is this concept of our thoughts. It might seem like no big deal. Hey, we have over 70,000 thoughts a day, so what's there to discuss?

But give it a second look. You'll begin to see just how powerful our thoughts and intentions can be, and what we can do to use them to our successful advantage.

Create By Design or By Default

Each day we create our life by the thoughts we have, the things we do, and the choices we make. So, why leave anything to chance? Rather than creating our outcomes by default, let's take our vision one step further.

You've identified your favorite ideas already, now let's put some $$ amounts to these goals. How much money would you really love to make?

It's okay to think big here. It's also a good idea to start with a smaller goal, beginning where you can with what you have, then working your way up from there.

Back to the idea of painting. Let's put some money progression goals to this:

- ✔ sell one of my paintings to a family member – $25
- ✔ create a website to market my paintings – $35
- ✔ sell my first painting to the public – $100
- ✔ have my artwork featured in a gallery – $500

In the example above, we started small and progressed our way up from there. Easiest first, then expand. A sale of your paintings to a family member is the most obvious place to start and you could probably earn anywhere between $25 and $100 on your first sale – depending on how generous your relatives are!

Next, we move up to offering additional paintings to more people via your own website. From there, we assume you will have some success and might begin selling your paintings also at weekend art shows to the general public. And after that, you might get invited to feature your work at a local gallery or in a private showing somewhere. Get the picture? Ha...thought you might like that one.

But seriously, there is no amount too small or too big. You are in charge and get to decide out of thin air the amount you wish to create.

Case Study Example – Mine!

In the introduction of this book, I told you about one of my first money-making ideas selling jewelry at the *DreamBuilder LIVE* event. The next time I was going to sell at this conference, I asked my Mom, "how can I make even more money this time? I don't want to just make $300, I want to make more!"

We brainstormed ideas of how to sell more products, but my Mom also taught me the power of "setting an intention" even without knowing the how. She told me that by simply setting my intention and goal, I don't have to immediately know how to make it happen. She said I can simply trust that either an idea, or an opportunity would literally show up to bring it forth.

TIP: You won't get the answer until you have a clear picture of the outcome of what you want in your own mind. And, to set a solid intention, write it down and say it out loud.

So, here's what happened next at the event. After I got there and set up, this time, my uncle's table was right next to my Mom's. He saw me doing such a good job of selling for my Mom's table, that he asked me to help him sell his CDs and books too. Wow!

Just like my Mom said, the opportunity to easily double my income at the event literally just showed up. Easy enough! But I also know that this opportunity came to me because I did exactly what my Mom said, I "set the intention" and spoke it out loud to my Mom.

I wrote it down (in the present tense as if I'd already reached my goal), and also believed it could happen, even though I didn't know how. I trusted and had faith (and did what I could with what I had).

NOTE: Your intention is basically a miniature version of your longer written vision.

I set my own intentions like this: *"I am so happy and grateful now that I have easily doubled my income at this event. This or something better, thank you..."*

Jet Fuel to Elevate Your Ideas

Let's go back once again to our notes and the dream vision you wrote out for your future. Now think about it. That right there, those written thoughts on that not so little piece of paper, holds your best ideas and goals – it's your very own vision blueprint.

I'm telling you, this way of thinking is so powerful, it can literally turn that piece of paper into an airplane ready for take-off. But just make a note that even the best jets need fuel, so make it a practice to read your vision out loud every day. Yes, out loud!

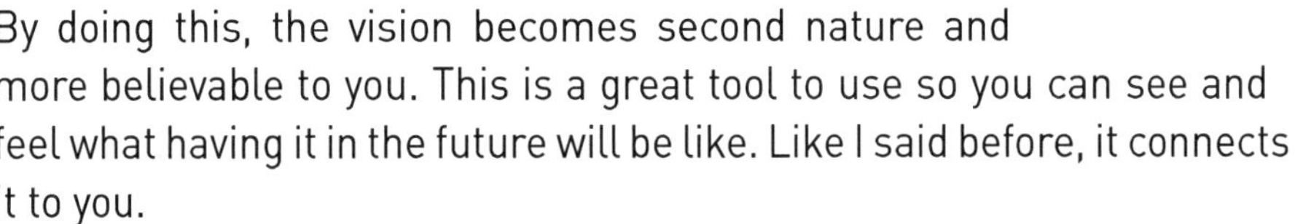

By doing this, the vision becomes second nature and more believable to you. This is a great tool to use so you can see and feel what having it in the future will be like. Like I said before, it connects it to you.

This way you can see and feel what having it (your dream come true) will be like. And when you practice that, soon enough it really will be in your pocket, hanging in your closet, parked in your driveway, or perhaps, helping others you've decided to help.

Vision Boards to Success:

Another thing you can do to enhance this process is to also make a vision board. What exactly is a vision board? Any pictures, photos, quotes, ideas, drawings, or anything else that reminds you of your vision goals. Kind of like a collage of your future.

For example, when I went to *DreamBuilder LIVE*, saying I wanted to make some more money other than with jewelry, I began to imagine doors opening and another opportunity to get dollars.

That was when my Uncle Mat needed help and my Grandma too. All of those are some "creating it in your mind" tools that can help you achieve your vision. The littlest things can make a huge difference.

For instance, I remember the time when my cousin had his graduation. On the block in front of the school was this girl and her Dad selling snacks, drinks, and graduation balloons. She was around 14 and it looked like they had been doing this same thing every year.

What a great idea, because hundreds of people walked right by their street to line up for the graduation. A built-in audience and they continued to build up their customer base each year. What she did was looked at a need around her and she filled it. It was an easy way for them to make extra cash and save people money.

Another common way kids make money is opening a babysitting business, a dog walking company, or selling sweets. And of course, the obvious lemonade stand. All these jobs are easy ways to earn some extra cash in a day.

Most don't take that much work, you can just go to the grocery store, pick up some supplies and then go out to your neighborhood and knock door-to-door, or set it up on a corner and make some money.

But for the babysitting or dog walking business, you would have to invest a little more time. Make some flyers and go put them around cars, on doorsteps, local cafés, Starbucks, or just about anywhere that you could put up a flyer.

It's pretty amazing what happens when you become clear in your focus and make specific intentions. It seems to breathe life into the kindling flames. It gives a clear idea of what it is that you want to have or have happen. Intentions are very specific.

And I'm not just talking about a list of to-do's, I'm talking about making some "I am..." statements. There is a real power behind anything that follows "I am."

A few "I am" statement examples:

- ✔ I am...fully capable of making my own money
- ✔ I am...a really good painter
- ✔ I am...being profitable as an artist

Don't those feel really powerful when you read them? Now, take it to a whole other level and say them out loud. Even more strength is generated, wouldn't you agree?

So even if it sounds corny, make it a habit to state your intentions out loud every morning and every night and see how quickly things begin to happen.

Go ahead! If you haven't already, write your vision now. Create your vision board to enhance it. Begin your vision with "I love..." and DON'T go on to the next chapter without finishing your written vision!

It can be as short as a paragraph...but better if it's a full page. Hey this is YOUR life and your money! Come on now. Would money want to come to your party if you don't put out a "welcome" mat in your own mind?

REMEMBER: I can show you the way towards making money, but your feet have to be the ones taking you down this path!!

End of Chapter Recap:

Again, think of answers to the following questions...

- ✔ How much money would I love to generate?
- ✔ What would I buy for either myself and/or others?
- ✔ How will this money help myself and/or others?
- ✔ Where would I like to make a contribution to help others, and what would that look like?

BONUS POINTS: Define "why" you want whatever it is you listed in the above exercise. Clearly define everything that motivates you to do what you plan on doing – making absolutely sure your answers align with your core values. Then take a moment to sit back and relax. Now in your mind, play the movie of YOU living your dream and accomplishing what you have written out in your very own vision.

Feel good? That's right...I'm going to suggest you do this at least once every day. Really! Successful people do this numerous times a day. This sort of repetition helps us come to believe in ourselves and take the steps that are required.

Good! Now, we are ready to move on to the next chapter and a new piece of the puzzle. And that is all about reaching out for support, and also looking inward to see what really makes us tick. Ready? Yes!

Part 2
REACH OUT
THE ART OF COLLABORATION

"A certain father had a family of sons, who were forever quarreling among themselves. No words he could say did the least good, so he cast about in his mind for some very striking examples that should make them see that discord would lead them to misfortune. One day when the quarreling had been much more violent than usual and each of the sons was moping in a surly manner, he asked one of them to bring him a bundle of sticks. Then handing the bundle to each of his sons in turn he told them to try to break it. But although each one tried his best, none was able to do so. The father then untied the bundle and gave the sticks to his sons to break one by one. This they did very easily. 'My sons,' said the father, 'do you not see how certain it is that if you agree with each other and help each other, it will be impossible for your enemies to injure you? But if you are divided among yourselves, you will be no stronger than a single stick in that bundle.' In unity is strength."

– The Bundle of Sticks

THE ART OF COLLABORATION

In This Chapter

- ✔ Taking an inventory of our beliefs and other intangibles
- ✔ Shining a light on things that try to block our success
- ✔ Tapping into the power of "when two or more are gathered..."

"IF YOU ARE A DREAMER, COME IN. IF YOU ARE A DREAMER, A WISHER, A LIAR. A HOPE-ER, A PRAY-ER, A MAGIC BEAN BUYER...IF YOU'RE A PRETENDER, COME SIT BY MY FIRE. FOR WE HAVE SOME FLAX-GOLDEN TALES TO SPIN. COME IN! COME IN!"
– SHEL SILVERSTEIN

The lesson we get from the story of the father and his sons, is that we are stronger when gathered together in unity. In other words, unity is the art of collaboration.

Much is gained from working with and trusting others in your journey towards success. And if we reach inward to improve ourselves, as we also reach out for the assistance of others, a dynamic team effort occurs.

In this chapter, not only will we explore the art of collaborating with others, but we'll also dive into the art of liberating our inner critic and negative voice. We'll see how the opinions of others may shape our thoughts and beliefs.

We will see that by gathering our resources and asking for help, we amplify our efforts towards a common goal (which creates more synergy and energy).

DOUBLE-CLICK YOUR RESOURCES

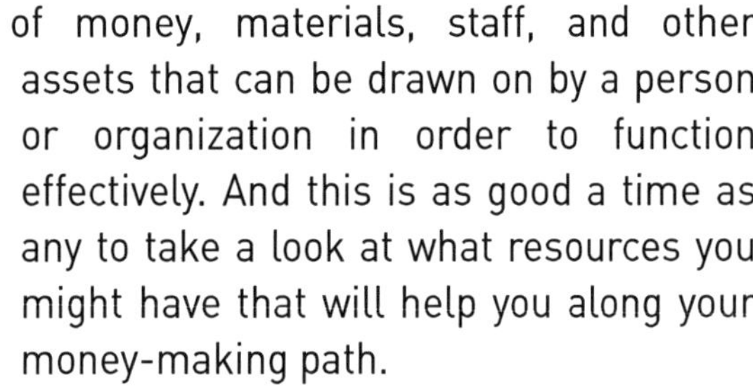

The definition of [re.source] is this: a stock or supply of money, materials, staff, and other assets that can be drawn on by a person or organization in order to function effectively. And this is as good a time as any to take a look at what resources you might have that will help you along your money-making path.

Some of your resources may be tangible things, like supplies, artwork, photographs, or physical stuff such as that. On the other hand, it could be more like your talents and any intellectual property sort of things you may have access to.

Who can you enlist to help you, mentor you, and support your ideas? What supplies, materials, and money might you need to get started initially? These are just some of the things to think about when starting out and moving forward with what you already have.

Go ahead. Start a list of all the materials and supplies you have now and everyone you know who can help. Look around and see what tools and materials you have at your disposal. Be sure your list shows what you have, and also what may be missing that you will need to get your hands on soon. For example:

- ✔ cooking supplies, pans, and an oven
- ✔ a catchy name for my baked goods stand
- ✔ my best friend loves to cook and will help
- ✔ my dad can help me set up the stand

Make sure you also make a list that includes those assets you have that are intangible, like knowing how to speak Spanish, or cooking skills, etc. (we will get more into those intangible things next).

TAKING INVENTORY

The Intangibles

"WE'RE JUST NORMAL PEOPLE TRYING TO DO WHAT WE LOVE AND FOLLOW OUR DREAMS."

– CARRIE UNDERWOOD

Not everything you need is tangible in a way that it can be held in your hands or stored in your garage. There are other things that are just as important in determining your eventual success.

And that is what we are going to focus on here in this chapter. Not the nuts and bolts material types of things, but intangible assets like people, partners, and mentors. But that doesn't excuse you from making that list of tangible resources mentioned above!

core Values

Before we reach out to see what family, friends, or teachers are at your disposal, first we are going to dive deeper into the one person that might just matter the most to your eventual success – YOU!

Yes, that's right. We are going to reach "in" before we reach out, and see what your heart says. Let's explore how your core values align with these business ideas. You can gather all the support in the world, but if you aren't feeling too positive about yourself, or what you are doing is not in alignment with who you are, you're eventually doomed before you even begin.

Core Values

Take a moment to check in with yourself and see what you are made of. While doing this, keep in mind your goals and what business success you'd like to achieve. Ask yourself these three questions:

- ✔ Who do others say I am?
- ✔ Who do I see myself as?
- ✔ What are my five most important attributes?

Be as honest as you can, and make sure to put in both the good and the bad. For some, the bad will come easy to list, and for others the good will be more accessible.

What you ideally want is a balance of both. If you see your list getting heavy on one side or the other, then sit a minute until you think of things to balance it out.

So let's take a look. Especially at the attributes. That's where your core values are going to show up first. Is it honesty? Cleverness? Artistic talent? Salesmanship skills? What are those things in life you value most?

REMEMBER: Keep these core values in mind when designing your money-making plans. It's important. You see, there is no amount of money that can buy "feeling good about yourself." So choose wisely and try to take the higher road whenever possible.

For example, if one of your core values is honesty, and one of your business ideas is to sell a product that you already know breaks easily, that's not 100% honest, is it? Ask yourself, how you'll feel about that if you go ahead and sell something like that?

Here's a list of core values that work for me. I try to follow them as best I can...but of course I'm not perfect. I'm a teenager. So, maybe you'd like to adopt (or at least consider) these values, and even try adding some of your own.

1. **Positive Attitude:** I try to stay positive regardless of what the outcome or result may be.
2. **Honesty:** I try my best to tell the truth and to do the "right thing" no matter what. This is a good North Star to follow.
3. **Respect:** I treat others as I'd want them to treat me. I try to show respect to myself and others.
4. **Determination:** I make my best effort to never give up and try my hardest.
5. **Gratitude:** I practice appreciating everything that has been given to me, such as my family, friends, and privileges.

Our "Limiting" Beliefs

Since the time we entered school, our minds have been sculpted to believe in society's brand; including beliefs that nobody is "good enough" and that you "have to have a lot of money." And let's not forget how you "need to be really smart or pretty." That's the formula we've been taught to believe ...maybe!!

I know you already are a success just by reading this book... and by setting goals and going out there with what you have. One thing every successful person agrees on is this: they were not a success when they got started... but they started anyway!

So, while you are dreaming up your vision and gathering your ideas on how to make your own money, make sure to always value your intangible assets. And keep doing what you can with what you already have.

IMPORTANT NOTE: TV and Radio ads have brainwashed us to think we will be happier if we have expensive toys and clothes and the things they are trying to sell us. Always remember that no THING is more valuable than the value of who you really are!

If you think being a famous rock star will make you happy because of all the money you are going to make, remember that not everything is as cool as it looks.

Everything that glitters is not gold. And maybe after looking at all the glitz and glamour, you might realize the ups and downs of being in the limelight and think to yourself, "That might not be very fun." Or you might decide instead, "Heck with the ups and downs, this is what I really want to do."

TIP: No one path is right or wrong, it's for you to decide what kind of person you want to be and what you want to create with your life.

Many people are just as happy with a Mustang as they are with a Jeep, so choose exactly what makes you happy and comfortable at the same time.

No two people are exactly alike, so dare to be unique. Carve out your own personal dream life by following your heart and going after your dream with everything you've got.

NEGATIVE VIBES

Voices of Doubt

"SURROUND YOURSELF WITH THE DREAMERS AND THE DOERS, THE BELIEVERS, AND THINKERS, BUT MOST OF ALL, SURROUND YOURSELF WITH THOSE WHO SEE GREATNESS WITHIN YOU, EVEN WHEN YOU DON'T SEE IT IN YOURSELF."

– SHEL SILVERSTEIN

Are you hearing any voices of doubt in your head, right now? If you are, that's okay. This is very normal and expected. The question is, "Will you listen to your doubts more than to your desires?"

Many times, the first thing that happens when we begin to daydream and imagine the life we'd love to live is that our negative voice pops into our ears and begins telling us all the reasons why it's not going to happen or that it's impossible for us to achieve or have those things for ourselves.

When this begins to happen, do whatever you can to turn off that negative voice inside your head. It's just basically saying the same thing over and over anyway, and telling you why you should not just go for it. Like in the cartoons when there's an angel and a devil sitting on each of your shoulders. Well, that negative voice is like the devil character, so don't be afraid to just flick him off and walk away.

Liberate That Negative Voice

Everybody has that voice of doubt inside, not just you. The president has that voice. Your teachers have that voice. Even famous singers and actors do too. Right before an audition that little voice of doubt can be telling them they have no chance of getting the role, that they are too shy to act, etc., etc. But the good ones don't let that voice get in the way. They follow their dreams and soon enough, get that role!

My goal is to support you in listening to the voice that supports your dreams. And did you know, the more you listen to that voice, the quieter the voice of doubt becomes? I suppose it never really goes away, but it does become a lot quieter with practice. I promise.

My Grandma taught my mom a tool when she was my age, and then my mom passed it along to me too. It's called the "take-it-back" technique. But the trick is, that first you need to learn to pay attention to what you are actually thinking about and saying to yourself. Once you begin doing this, you will be able to use this trick to stop that "doubting Thomas" and instead, listen to the voice of your dreams.

So here it is. Anytime something negative pops into your head, like, "I can't afford that," or "I can't do this," push the pause button in your mind, and tell that doubting thought, "Cancel-cancel." Then re-state that in the positive (making sure it's in the present tense).

In other words, switch it up to say something like, "A way to afford this is going to show up any day" or, "I will find a way to do it." This is the "take-it-back" technique. You take the power back from your doubt, and hand it over to your dream. It's like installing a new way of thinking.

Try it...this really works.

Circle of Support

Not only do we have to turn down the volume on the voice of doubt, but we have to notice those around us too. It is important to surround yourself with true supporters. Just because they are your family and friends who love you, that doesn't mean they don't have their own fears and hang-ups that can get in the way of believing in and supporting your dreams.

It is probably a good idea to only share your ideas and goals with a few people who you can really trust your dreams with. Like a brand new iPhone without a case, you wouldn't want to hand it off to just anybody would you? Make sure those you share your ideas with, are also positive and supportive people.

How do you know who to trust? Well, a great way is to observe and learn how they are within their own lives. Do they follow their hearts and go after their own dreams? Or do they live inside a "safe" box?

Follow your HEART

Continue to learn and notice by really listening to the way they talk. Do they use positive encouraging words? Or do they use "can't" or "don't" a lot of the time? Trust your gut instincts and share your dreams with those who will truly support your vision.

Take a minute right now and think of at least one person you can trust with your dream. Some ideas are to start with your mom, dad, uncle, church minister, teacher, or coach. And maybe, a good friend only if they are open to being a dreamer too. We will get back to this shortly, in the "partners in believing" part, just a few sections ahead of where we are now.

DISCARD AND DESERVE

It's as good a time as any to dig deeper into the aspects of paradigms and see how they can control the ways we behave during our interactions with others. The Merriam-Webster's definition for paradigm is:

"A philosophical and theoretical framework of a scientific school or discipline within which theories, laws, and generalizations and the experiments performed in support of them are formulated; broadly: a philosophical or theoretical framework of any kind."

What the heck is that all about? In layman's terms, a paradigm is simply a mental program, the way we see the world. Like wearing a pair of glasses. The lens affects how we see everything else. Paradigms are created by what our parents teach us, what our schools teach us, and what we pick up from the media, etc. And for the purpose of our discussion here, I want to dive into the ways that paradigms mold our way of thinking.

PARA-WHAT?

Blocking Your Success

"YOU CAN ONLY HAVE THAT WHICH YOU BELIEVE YOU DESERVE — THAT WHICH YOU CAN ACTUALLY SEE YOURSELF HAVING. ANYTHING IS POSSIBLE, BUT FIRST YOU MUST BELIEVE IT IN YOURSELF."

– MARY MORRISSEY

Have you heard the saying, "Change your thinking, change your life?" Well, how about "Change your paradigms, change your life." Para-whats? They are funny little creatures that can be really hard to get rid of completely. Sometimes we think they've moved on, only to realize they were just hiding behind some bushes. Paradigms tend to show up at the most inconvenient times and have great disguises that make you think they've actually gone away.

So since they are very, very sneaky...don't be so hard on yourself if you fall prey to this sort of roadblock. When you find yourself stopping short of your goal, or find that something is always getting in your way, take a moment to dig deeper and see if it might be your sneaky little paradigms at work instead.

Excuses and Conditions

Have you ever noticed your thoughts? The judging, criticizing, negative ones. Those times when we reject an idea, give ourselves reasons, or excuses, or look to the conditions we are faced with as to why we can't do something (or why it's not at all possible)?

What a great example of when those pesky paradigms are kicking in... again. How many times have you heard your friends complain about why they can't do something? And by that I mean slipping into excuses and conditions... looking at all the reasons why it won't happen or can't happen.

If I said there is an invisible bank with an infinite supply of money and that all the money in the entire world is available to you, would you believe me??? Would you agree, and say, "Okay yeah, that's 100% true?" Or would reasons or conditions start popping up in your mind to suggest that the idea is crazy and untrue?

Most people fall into the "that's crazy" way of thinking, but the reality is, that way of thinking comes mostly from the opinions of what other people have said, taught, or have passed down to you in the past.

Remember, as crazy as it sounds now, there was a time when people believed the world was flat and no one would ever walk on the moon.

TIP: Don't buy into the lack of mentality and limitations of others... there is way more available to you than you might think. Seriously.

The Power of Your Thoughts

This isn't the first time I've talked about how our thoughts have the power to fuel our dreams. But since it is so important, I will dive into this a little bit more. Why, you ask? Because it's better to be driving through life with the power of a Ferrari instead of riding in a horse and buggy.

Like I've said before, our thoughts are powerful. So strong in fact, that if we're not careful, we might end up letting them control our day-to-day lives. Believe me, we can choose to be happy (and ignore the reasons to not be happy). Or, we can let our thoughts make us sad, depressed, or angry. It's up to us. We really are a sum of our thoughts, you know.

We become what we allow ourselves to become. When someone has no way of seeing a better way of living, only the basic school, college, job, life, they tend to just give up or many times hold themselves back.

Bottom line is that we can't let anybody else's thinking control ours. That is a power we should keep for ourselves. Oh yeah, and remember we can control our Subway orders too, of course. Ha-ha.

Anyways, it always stuns me to see how many people let money control their lives. "I don't have the money for this... or that." Pretty common actually. Whether you can afford it or not should never be thought about or debated.

Every time you make a solid decision on what it is you really want (and I'm telling you... I see it happening every time) the puzzle starts putting itself together and the money just seems to show up.

That, my friend, is the power of our thoughts!

STAND IN YOUR STRENGTH

Self-Esteem and Confidence

"DON'T LET THE OPINIONS OF THE AVERAGE PERSON SWAY YOU. DREAM, AND THEY THINK YOU'RE CRAZY. SUCCEED, AND THEY THINK YOU'RE LUCKY. ACQUIRE WEALTH, AND THEY THINK YOU'RE GREEDY. PAY NO ATTENTION. THEY SIMPLY DON'T UNDERSTAND."

– ROBERT G. ALLEN

Do you think we're born with confidence and self-esteem? Or do you think that maybe it grows out of our experiences and adventures? To me, the more success we have, the more these qualities grow.

Just the same, if we let others get to us, we can have our self-esteem and confidence torn down or stripped away, just by caring too much about what others think or say... which can be destructive to our potential.

This is a big, big, big one for most of us. We listen to and value the opinions of others. In some cases, this is perfectly fine. But in other cases, it can be destructive and hold us back from being the best we can be and from achieving success. Maybe others mean well, but at the end of the day, whose opinion matters most?

If we don't install a virus protector, this can be a big problem. We've been taught that our sense of value or self-worth is based on outside things like popularity, grades, the clothes we wear, or our looks. But it's not! I'm here to tell you... none of that stuff matters!

All that really matters is how you feel about yourself. That's the most important ingredient to success. If you see your success and stand in that strength, others will see you this way too.

If someone says something negative to you, or you think a negative thought about yourself, remember to use the "take-it-back" technique. Replace the voice of doubters with the voice of your dreams.

When something negative pops into your head, like, "I can't afford this," or "I'm so stupid," or "That's too hard, I can't do that," push the pause button by saying..."Cancel-cancel."

Never Enough

Since we are on the subject of negativity and doubters, let's make a quick mention of the mistake many kids fall into, and that's the belief that there is never enough. There is not enough money to go around. There is not enough money to do what I want to do. There is never enough time. There is no way to do what I want to do... are you getting the point?

TIP: Stay clear from those types of people while you build your money-making ideas. Why make it any harder than it needs to be, right?

Or, once you accomplish something or get to your goal, you always want more or something else. It's easy to see this with clothes and things like gadgets where we always want the latest and greatest.

And, have you ever noticed how some people are always chasing the dream and not living their dreams? The truth is as soon as we buy the new clothes or toys, they are "used" the next day, and usually not nearly as great as we thought they'd be.

Another example is, we dream about going on vacation and think about all the fun we are going to have. There's all the planning, shopping, packing to do before we go. Then while we are on vacation, how many times do we catch ourselves thinking about how we miss our friends and pets back home?

The point is to try and enjoy what you are doing when you are doing it, or you'll miss so much of real life along the way. The trick is to have an "attitude of gratitude" and be grateful for what we already have.

Who's Controlling Who?

So let's take a minute to think about this a little more. Who is really controlling who? Are you driving your thoughts, or are other people doing more of this work for you? Are you, or is someone else, sitting in the driver's seat making the decisions?

It's time for all of us to break the cycle of limiting beliefs. It is time for each one of us to elevate our thoughts, dreams and desires and to go for it. Here is an interview I did with someone who did just that:

1. **What is your business, and what's the purpose of it?** My company is MySocialCloud.com. It's an online password vault that allows users to store all their usernames and passwords and automatically log into anything that requires one without typing it in. MySocialCloud eliminates the need for people to remember and type in usernames and passwords.

2. How old were you at the time? What made you want to start? I was 18 years old and had just graduated high school when my brother and I started MySocialCloud. My brother had a spreadsheet with all his usernames and passwords, but once his computer crashed – he lost that spreadsheet along with everything else on his computer. We decided that it was time the world had a place online that stored all this information so that people would never lose the pieces of paper they wrote their passwords on, etc.

3. What steps did you take to achieve it? Did you use any special creation type tools? First I moved to Los Angeles with my brother after I graduated high school – to be away from the hustle and bustle of life back home and to work full time on bringing our idea to fruition. That summer, I spent a lot of time on market research and business planning while my brother and our other team member, Shiv, built the initial prototype (working version of our site). Later that summer, I saw a tweet from Sir Richard Branson that said, "Come meet me in Miami for intimate cocktails, donate $2,000.00 to charity through this email address." I responded immediately and said that my brother and I would love to come meet Sir Richard in Miami (even though we weren't old enough to drink cocktails). Someone on his staff emailed back and said that we were more than welcome to come – as long as we could donate the $2,000.00 each to charity and be in Miami in 48 hours. So my brother and I did the only thing we could think to do at the time to get the $4,000.00, which was call up our Mom and Dad to see if they'd loan us the money. After our Dad made us write a business proposal as to how we would use the money and how we planned to pay him back, our parents lent us the money and we flew to Miami. We were able to meet Sir Richard Branson, tell him about ourselves and ask for his contact details. We went back to Los Angeles and finished our prototype and within the month, we were able to send the prototype to Richard. He introduced us to Jerry Murdock, who then flew out to Los Angeles to meet us. That night, Jerry took us out to dinner and said that he and Richard would invest just about $1mil in the company. After that, we used the money to keep developing our product, build out our website and the browser extensions that help MySocialCloud run. We expanded our team to 10 people and kept developing our product and pushing it out to new users and customers. We also began building relationships to start rolling out our username and password management product to enterprise companies.

4. **How much money did you make? And what advice would you give other young entrepreneurs?** A company by the name of Reputation.com just acquired MySocialCloud (meaning they bought out our technology and IP). The amount is not being announced as Reputation.com is still a private company. My advice would be to talk to as many people as possible about an idea you have and get as much feedback as you can. Remember that constructive criticism is better than praise, as it allows you to refine your vision and fix your product for better use.

Isn't that an awesome story? It is one of a zillion success stories out there. Which leads me to share one of my own personal dreams... I want this book and the information I'm sharing with you to help you succeed. I really hope that with this information, you will be able to both recognize the paradigm blocks that may be getting in your way and to move past them so you can achieve great success stories of your own.

So get going...I want to see you on that other side of limited thinking and I want us to meet each other in the winners circle of success. Woo hoo! I can see it now!!!

DEVELOP YOUR RELATIONSHIPS

Develop your RELATIONSHIPS

Okay, here's a risky move. I'm gonna let my mom in for a quick "parent-to-parent" bit of advice! Don't call me out... just go with me on this. The first step of building a support team around you is to get buy-in from your parents. Trust me, this will all go much better if you and your mom and dad are on the same page. So, please pass this note along to them...

NOTE FROM MY PARENTS TO YOURS: *It's very important to help your child dream big and wide. The practice for us, as parents, is to NOT chop down their ideas with comments like..."You aren't old enough," "We don't have the time or money for that idea"...*

Instead, you can say..."I love how creative you are being, and how well you are using your imagination." "Okay, so let's start right where you are with what you have – and let's write down 10 things you can do right where you are now to move in this direction."

For example, let's say your child's dream is to open their own restaurant. Instead of saying..."You're not old enough," or "Are you crazy? Restaurants lose money and we can't afford a risk like that."

Instead, you could say, "Okay, that's great. What can we do right now, with what we have or who we know to move in that direction?" The idea is to encourage your child to source at least 20 ways that they could start.

One idea might be to invite some friends and family over and create an "in-house" restaurant in your own home, complete with a mini menu to order from. It could be a few items your teen can easily make using your own kitchen. They can take orders, cook, and serve up the food... then present the bill, receive a tip, and clean up the mess.

This will provide the real feeling of what owning a restaurant is like, using the resources they have available to them right now. And by supporting your teen in this manner, they will most likely feel safe to share future dreams with you. Now that's a win-win!

Just make sure you don't slip into that limited way of thinking that produces statements like, "I just want to protect them from getting hurt or getting their hopes up only to be let down." Encourage your teens to do more, to try new ideas and expand. A little bit of falling down here and there never hurt anyone, it only helps to make you stronger and more determined.

CREATING A SUPPORT SYSTEM

Force Field Shield (aka Virus Protector)

> "CHANGING YOURSELF TO FIT WHAT YOU THINK OTHER PEOPLE WANT DOESN'T WORK."
>
> – MARY MORRISSEY

At times, it can be useful to have a sort of protective force field like the invisible shields you see used in the movies when aliens are attacking or something like that. Our dreams need to be protected from invasions of the mind-hackers out there.

Many times, it's not even from enemies or whatever, it comes innocently from your friends and family who care about you. I'm not saying they are doing anything maliciously, but just the same, sometimes even though they mean well, they can be stealing away the fuel and desire of your dreams.

Mind Invasions

This is where we need to be mindful of what we allow into our heads. The operating systems of computers are vulnerable to attacks, and that's why we get virus protectors installed. The same goes for our minds (both the conscious and sub-conscious). This is where it is important to protect ourselves from the loads of negativity and negative influences that are knocking at the door and trying to get in.

You must not let other people's ideas about money invade your mind. Don't let them hack into your operating system and take your power. Ignore them, especially classmates or your friends, when they are not being as supportive as you need them to be.

Even without trying, they can hurt your dream's feelings. If they reject or shun an idea, if people don't believe in you, or they say "no", don't let that answer be your "no" (unless of course it really is something you should be saying "no" to – like something dangerous!).

If you really want something or you propose an offer or idea and they don't give it or take it from you, don't let that stop you. There are other options. Invest your energy in persistence. And, don't just agree with their terms and conditions. Write your own conditions and edit theirs if need be.

What Goes Around Comes Around

Have you ever heard that saying before? Or know how a boomerang works? Well, if you give out the negative energy of anger, greed, envy, and selfishness, that is what you'll get back. Including, a low flow of money.

On the other hand, if you give off positive, open, and giving energy...the world will open many doors for you. Even open doors leading to that pot of gold at the end of the rainbow.

My mom told me a story once, about how she was at a conference selling her products and her table was in the very back corner of the room. Even before the event started, she began to feel bad because she had the worst spot in the whole room.

She worried that no one was going to see her and buy any of her products. Hour after hour, she felt worse and worse. And actually, no one was visiting her table. So, she decided to change her attitude. First she decided to focus on being grateful for the opportunity of being at the event.

Then, any time her mind wanted to worry or complain, she decided to use the power of her imagination to watch a make-believe movie in her mind. In this movie, lots of people were buying, and being helped by her products and services. Her customers were happy, and she was feeling grateful.

Even though nothing had actually changed at her table yet, her attitude changed. By watching this movie in her mind, it helped her begin to feel better inside.

Then you know what happened next? Within an hour of shifting her attitude from complaining, worry and fear, to an attitude of gratitude, people did start to magically visit her booth. Before she knew it, she had sold a lot of products.

SPECIAL NOTE: Whatever you are doing, watch your thoughts and your attitudes. Always strive to...

- ✔ Notice the good in yourself and others
- ✔ Be grateful for what you do have and can do
- ✔ Find the opportunity in every situation

My mom told me that the moral of her story was, "What you think = what you attract." And I can see that this really is the truth of how things work.

Your Words Hold Power and Energy

Did you know the most successful people make it a practice to never say what they "don't want" or "can't do." Whatever you say (and truly believe deep down inside) is what you make happen. This means, if you say you can't, then you can't. This language causes an attitude of failure.

TIP: Eliminate the words "don't" and "can't" from your vocabulary. It makes a huge difference!

What successful people tend to say is, what they do want and can do. For example, if I say, "I will not give up," even though it seems like a positive attitude, my brain actually hears, "Give up." So the better response is, "I will give it my all" or "I will succeed."

These kinds of statements create a successful attitude. Here are a few examples of how to flip these thoughts and statements around into the positive:

Negative = "Don't forget to..." =→
Positive = "Today I will remember to ... "

Negative = "I don't want to get a bad grade" =→
Positive = "I'm getting a good grade"

Negative = "I am really bad at..." =→
Positive = "With practice and persistence every day I am getting better at..."

Negative = "I'm so stupid" =→
Positive = "I am smart and I learn more each and every day!"

Take a moment now to reflect and write out a few things you normally say that are from a negative point of view. Then write out the positive words you will put in place of those negative words.

Here's another great thing to do. Write this positive statement down and tape it to your bathroom mirror or on the inside of your locker:

"Today I am a person who is honest and persistent, who puts my values first and shows up as my best self with confidence!"

Then be sure to engrave this statement into your heart and soul:

"There are many teens who have achieved their money goals. I can be one too!"

Practice never being too arrogant or having low self-esteem. Self-confidence comes through learning from your mistakes, dedicating yourself to succeed, and trying new things. So be sure to practice staying positive in everything you do.

PARTNERS IN BELIEVING

Real Support

"WHEN YOU WORK WITH OTHERS YOU CAN ACCOMPLISH WAY MORE THAN TRYING TO ACCOMPLISH THINGS ON YOUR OWN. ASKING FOR HELP WILL AMPLIFY YOUR EFFORTS."

—ALLIE JOY

This is where we take a look at who's got your back and who can assist you towards reaching your goals. My Grandma taught me a principle called "partners in believing." Whether it's from peers or parents, we all have those we look to for advice and reassurance.

And sometimes it is these very people who we need to turn to when our confidence is shy. Sometimes it's believing in their belief that you can do something that will get you through the rough spots and past the finish line of your dreams.

Select Your D.R.E.A.M. Team

Do you already have a "buddy in believing?" Someone who doesn't dampen your dream, but instead lifts you up? If you don't have one, let's think for a minute and come up with some candidates for the job. Is there someone in your life now, either a relative, a teacher, or coach, who you already know believes in you?

Think of one to three adults who could fill this role. Write down at least one person you can trust with your dream. Here are some ideas...your mom, dad, uncle, church minister, teacher, or coach. Or maybe a good friend, but only if they are capable of being a dreamer too. Ask at least one adult if they will be your support partner as you move forward towards your dreams.

DREAM Team

Also, it's equally important to be a buddy in believing for someone else. Think of three friends or relatives whom you can believe in and support as well. Write down their names and why you believe in them. Send a friend you know a text message letting them know you believe in them.

REMEMBER: What goes around, comes around, right?

One of the most popular books on success, "Think and Grow Rich" by Napoleon Hill, states that one of biggest factors of being successful is the principle of creating a "mastermind". In the book he writes, the mastermind is when two or more people work well together towards the same goal.

For me, I have been very blessed to receive the help, aka mastermind, of my family. At first my mastermind was my mom. Then my Grandma and my dad joined, and we then had many people helping support me in writing this book. We will dive more into how important mentors and masters are in Chapter 3.

So now it's your turn to think about your family and friends, plus other people who you know support you and believe in you. In addition to your partner in believing, is there anyone else you can add to this list?

Decide who you think your mastermind group will be. You need at least one or two other people to be on your team. I'm going to have you call this your D.R.E.A.M. Team! To be really successful and reach your goals, whether it's an extra $20 or $2,000, you need the help of others, you need the help of a D.R.E.A.M. Team.

You won't be nearly as successful if you try to go at it alone. Build a support team. Take a moment now and on a piece of paper write down who you would like to join your D.R.E.A.M. Team. Now write down when you are going to talk to them about joining your team. Don't put it off. I'd suggest calling or talking to them about it today!

Enthusiasm Is Contagious

Once you've chosen those people you can trust with your dream and the ideas that light you up, you will begin to see how your enthusiasm catches on with everyone around you.

They too will feel your energy and that creates even more energy in them. And before you know it, you'll have a team of supporters in your court. All of you will basically be buzzing with energy and the electricity will be contagious.

On the other hand, if you pursue something that you have only lukewarm feelings about (or even worse, don't really want to do at all), then others will feel that energy as well. And again, before you know it, you'll feel like your shoes are stuck in quicksand or are caked with mud and are as heavy as bricks.

TIP: Avoid this lackluster route at all costs.

Like I said already, it's important to schedule a time today or this week to sit down with your D.R.E.A.M. Team (whether that's you and your partner in believing, or you and several other people). Together, you want to inventory everything you already have access to and everyone you know and they know, who could help you accomplish your goals.

It might be surprising to see how many combined resources you already have. Most likely, everything you really need is sitting right under your nose.

A good example of this is my Uncle Mat. He and his best friend, Jason, were high school football players and wanted to make some extra cash. They came up with the idea of doing a sports training camp called Quickness Camp where they trained junior high and high school football players over the summer to get them ready for the upcoming season.

They went to the store to buy the equipment needed and realized it was very expensive... more money than they had combined. So, they did some research and found a guy who worked as a speed and fitness coach nearby who could potentially be a great resource.

They went to talk with him despite the fact that he might turn them down because they could be seen as his competition. But this trainer saw their passion and determination, and let them borrow some of the equipment he wasn't using.

Like I've said, if you walk around with your passion shining and have a burning desire for your dream, people will be more than willing to help you.

End of Chapter Recap:

Take a few minutes to do the following "reaching out" and collaborative activities that will help you reach your money goals:

- ✔ Ask at least one person if they will be your support partner as you move forward.
- ✔ Write down all of the resources you already have or need to bring forth your money goals.
- ✔ Think of other people, friends, or adults who might have the resources to help you, and be willing to support your money goals.

And, remember to use the "take-it-back" technique as often as necessary.

Basically, you just need to re-state what you love about yourself, in the present tense. Like "I am confident! I am smart! I can do this! I've got what it takes!"

Negative = "I can't do it" = → Cancel-Cancel
Positive = "As I practice every day I see myself easily getting better and better!"

BONUS POINTS: What are some things you know you say to yourself that are critical and not supportive? Write down three things, then restate them as we did in the exercise above. By the way, you will get really good at this over time...and the handcuffs of doubt and the shackles of fear will lose their grip. Actually, it's quite fun as you get power over those doubts. Now to get back to some positive mojo, go ahead and also write down five qualities you like about yourself. Wow, now doesn't that make you feel much better??

Part 3

ENDEAVOR

THE ART OF TAKING ACTION

"If one advances confidently in the direction of his dreams, and endeavors to live the life which he has imagined, he will meet with a success unexpected in common hours. He will put some things behind, will pass an invisible boundary; new, universal, and more liberal laws will begin to establish themselves around and within him; or the old laws be expanded, and interpreted in his favor in a more liberal sense, and he will live with the license of a higher order of beings. In proportion as he simplifies his life, the laws of the universe will appear less complex, and solitude will not be solitude, nor poverty poverty, nor weakness weakness. If you have built castles in the air, your work need not be lost; that is where they should be. Now put the foundations under them."

– Henry David Thoreau

THE ART OF TAKING ACTION

In This Chapter

- ✔ Propelling our dreams into the higher stratospheres
- ✔ Planning for success and learning how to make solid decisions
- ✔ Peeking inside to what fears may be holding us back

"NOTHING WILL HAPPEN WITHOUT ACTION. CREATE AND FOLLOW A PLAN. YOU'RE GOING TO GET A RESULT. IT MAY NOT BE PERFECT BUT AT LEAST YOU HAVE STARTED."

– BOB PROCTOR

And that's it. Getting started. Advancing confidently in the direction of your dreams. Creating momentum. Nothing will ever happen if we never begin. No idea gets implemented if you never take the first step.

In order to reach our "money-making" goals, we need to do what we can with what we already have. That begins with the use of our imagination, then expands through our beliefs (or contracts with *limited* ones).

During this expansion phase, we again use the power of our mind: this time by taking action. We do this even while facing our biggest (or littlest) fears as our faith becomes stronger.

In this chapter, we will learn how to face our fears and focus on our desires to overcome what we don't know or don't have in order to reach our goals. We will also see that taking action one step at a time (even if we are afraid) will create positive momentum to help us move in the direction of our dreams. We will explore how making solid decisions will help determine what the next steps should be to lead us to success.

DREAM INTO EXISTENCE

Going back to the movie, *Inception*, let's look deeper into what's real and what's not... what are dreams and what is reality? Sometimes, it's hard to know for sure. But what if we put our name on the dream?

You've probably heard this said before, "Change your thinking, change your results." Well, what if we train our minds to make sure our dreams come true?

Believe me, it is possible. Dreams do come true. This I know from personal experience. And it's as easy as changing the channel on your TV remote.

Once you make a decision to follow a dream, and set your intentions in motion, it's like magic. I'm telling you, the results just show up to become your reality. But I'm getting ahead of myself. First, let's take a look at collecting, sorting, and selecting our ideas.

VACUUM EFFECT

Reeling In the Thoughts

"IDEAS ARE LIKE SLIPPERY FISH; THEY HAVE A PECULIAR KNACK FOR GETTING AWAY FROM US UNLESS WE GAFFE THEM ON THE POINT OF A PENCIL."

– EARL NIGHTINGALE

Here is a process that works well for sourcing ideas and brainstorming. It's a great method to gather up ideas around any activity or project you might have in mind. It also gives us the freedom to not worry about what the idea looks like at first and gives us permission to sound dumb. In this process, it's okay to gather up all ideas whether they make sense or not. Make no judgments now. Just write down every idea that shows up for organizing or throwing out later.

Oh, and here is an important point to remember. When you actually write down all those ideas you are reeling in, you have literally created a vacuum for your genius to flow through. You are pulling to you, the ideas for the materials, resources, and people to come help you achieve your dream. Kind of like a magnet.

Bring Along the Fishing Net

If we really allow ourselves the freedom to do this, can you imagine the ideas our net will now catch that otherwise might have been missed?

Never be afraid of scooping up all ideas to begin with... the big ones, the little ones, the pretty ones, and also what appear to be the ugly ones too. All of them are useful at this point, so collect each and every one.

Let's practice our "fishing" skills. And to do this we will illustrate by using an imagined desire of going to a *One Direction concert* (or maybe it's the *Super Bowl*). The thing is, either we don't have the cash or the tickets are all sold out. On the surface, it might look like you can't go, right? So, what's next?

Can we dream our way to this event? The correct answer is YES. But, it's easier for me to show you than to tell you. So, let's begin by writing down all the ideas that pop into our head of what we could do to go to this event. Some of them will be crummy, and some of them will be good, but let's just put down every idea that we can think of for now.

The main point here is to remember that the person who lives the life where their "mom is not their money" is the person who has moved into a belief that there *has* to be a way for me to go to that concert or game. The very fact that the desire exists means there is a real (and scientific) way to achieve that goal.

This brings us to something really important. And that is, the brainstorming vs. dream building thing. This is also something I learned from my Grandma.

There is a real difference between the two. Anyone can brainstorm and have an idea or a list of ideas, but real "dream building" relies on "if I have the desire, then there *has to be a way* to achieve it."

So the first thing to do would be to move into a belief that there has to be a way to generate the money, so I can go to that concert or game. I don't know what that is right now, but the fact that I even want to go means there is a way to do it.

And since we are now "dream builders" here and not just your ordinary brainstormers, let's move on with that in mind.

A Barometer for Your Desires

Now this is a biggie. The "why" is a huge motivator towards getting your goals accomplished. If there is no real fire behind your motivation, then again your actions will be lukewarm (or less). But if the why is so big that you can't think of anything else except getting this goal, you'll have fire under those coals that will keep your dream burning hot.

Going back to going to the concert/game example, on a scale from 1 to 10, how much do you want this? Why is this important? Well, if it's not a "burning" desire, if you don't *REALLY* want to go to the concert/game, you're not going to generate all of the ideas that will give you the answers you need. You'll just be lukewarm. And, the thing is, if you are lukewarm about your dreams or goals, you'll be lukewarm in the ideas that you generate for it.

If you have a goal that is a burning desire, but don't know yet HOW to make it happen (in regards to creating your plan of attack) here's something you can start with. The first thing I'm going invite you to do, is really *FEEL* what it's going to be like to attend the concert.

How does it feel? Well let's begin by imagining in your mind all the flashing lights, screaming fans, and that star-struck rush you get the minute the band walks on stage. Hear the music and you are singing right along with them. Really imagine this and how it feels.

Something REALLY important you will need to know is that we are often playing little movies in our own minds. This is normal. And it is happening all the time. So use this powerful "imagination tool" to help you become successful in your money-making ideas or business, and use it to your advantage.

So, how close do you want your seats to be? Front row? Center maybe? Okay, front row and center. Just close enough so you can make eye contact with the lead singer (and who can touch your outstretched hands). See it in your mind...and fill in every last detail you can imagine.

Write it all down. And remember, even if your ideas are only on paper right now, that's where it all begins. Soon you will see that the very act of writing this down gives it more power, and what is on paper tends to come to life right in front of your own eyes.

Case Study Example - Mine Again...

If you are able to *feel* the energy of what your imagined life will be (when you say yes to anything you want), you can achieve many great goals. So, go ahead and put on your dreams like they were an outfit and see how they feel. Even go as far as to cut out pieces of paper, color them green, and count them every day, as if it was real money and it was already yours.

Try any exercise you choose that works for you, like doodling something that stands for your vision every day. Or writing it on your hand, a special little symbol that only you can recognize, and looking at it all throughout the day. These things actually work.

One time I did just that and didn't even realize what I was doing. During the week leading up to cheerleading tryouts, I would doodle little cheer stick figures and write "cheer" around my paper. I also talked about how it would be once I made it on the team with my friends.

In other words, I was *feeling* how it would feel making the team. I imagined myself remembering the whole dance and cheers, all five of them. Then when it came time for my friends and I to try out, we had a great time and all of us ended up making the team!

Like I said above, the very act of writing this down gives it more power, and what you put on paper comes to life right before your very own eyes.

LADDER OF SUCCESS

The Big Leap

"GO CONFIDENTLY IN THE DIRECTION OF YOUR DREAMS. LIVE THE LIFE YOU HAVE IMAGINED."
– HENRY DAVID THOREAU

The more feelings and life you breathe into your goals through visualization, using the colors of your imagination, the more electricity that will be put into them. And, the more electricity they have, the faster you will get to the top of that ladder of success.

This may be difficult to grasp at first, but just know it's all backed up by science. As Thoreau said so well, "Go confidently in the direction of your dreams...live the life you imagined." In other words, go for it!

Possibility to Probability

Let's keep it simple. Take the first steps...feel how it feels, and then you say to yourself, now what could I do to make that possible? The key is to be open to the possibilities and build a belief that I can't have the desire without there being a way for it to happen.

You will not just be dreaming, or praying, but you will tap into what it feels like to be living your burning desire. Then, through your imagination, you will be given ideas you can act on that will help you get there.

The act of moving it from possibility to probability to predictability is science. It's like climbing up one rung of the ladder at a time. And that's what I am helping you do here. Helping you believe that there is one idea or several ideas strung together, that can make this dream or desire happen.

You mean that this could *really* happen? YES!!

Do you believe it's possible? And that it could really happen? I certainly do! You only need to get that inside your head and believe it's possible. Or at least believe that I *believe* it is not only possible, but it's probable. Simply borrow my believing power, or the power of someone who loves you, to help you along until your own belief is stronger.

Burning Desires

I said this above, if it's not a burning desire, you'll be lukewarm about the results, and lukewarm on the ideas to generate that income to get what you desire.

But if you tap into the passion that is driving you towards your goal, there is no limit to where you take this dream. You can climb the ladder to the top rung.

Think of it like this. In your imagination, you went all the way from just wanting to go to a concert (or the Super Bowl), to *going* to the concert, to actually being right smack in the middle of the front row!

You can't help it but have your entire body's energy shift when you get that far into the *feeling* of being there like that. You begin to feel the possibilities, and have engaged your emotions because you are having a real *experience* of it in your imagination.

Okay, so maybe it's not as *real* as if you were actually in the front row, but for just a flash of a moment, you can have that feeling. And that's where the magic comes in!

Take it a step further to the day after the concert/game, when you wake up and remember all the things you saw. Your ears are still ringing from all the screaming, and you just found some nacho cheese on your arm. Electricity still runs through your body because it was way better than you expected.

This is the feeling you want to memorize because it's a magnet for the ideas that'll help you find your way. You've got to be in the picture... not just outside the picture, but inside it. A lot of people miss that part and that's the magic to having things happen... fast.

DECIDE ON A PLAN

You know how I keep saying you can either run a mile or a marathon? Which do you choose? Well the cool thing is that you get to decide. You get to choose what direction and course you take. Just make sure to always make your decisions with the end in mind, then work backwards with a solid plan of attack.

Always keep in mind, there is money basically everywhere you look. You just need to keep your eyes open. Support that idea and that way of thinking and you'll find hidden possibilities and opportunities lying just under the surface... and waiting to be found.

All you need to do is to make a decision even without knowing the "how." You begin by deciding on what it is that you want, then move forward by taking the first steps you can and with what you already have.

LITTLE STEPS

Dreams and Visions

"REACH OUT TO THE PEOPLE YOU KNOW TO ABSOLUTELY HELP YOU RECOGNIZE THAT THERE'S SOMETHING GREAT INSIDE OF YOU AND THE GIFT YOU HAVE TO GIVE. IT'S NOT DEPENDENT ON AGE, MONEY, OR EDUCATION."
– MARY MORRISSEY

We've talked a lot about dreams and visions, but when you seek success, you can never do too much of that or too often. I've also shown examples (and more case studies are to come) of the kids who have taken their dreams and turned them into million dollar enterprises.

So what do these kids have that most kids don't have? Here's a hint. It has nothing to do with their age, where they were born, how much money their parents have, or how smart they are. A great imagination is the #1 thing and common denominator. The good news is we are all born with it!

And once these kids successfully tapped into and used their imaginations, they didn't stop there.

Here are the main steps they followed (and good news, we've already finished the first four):

- ✔ they **Dreamed** big – and chose an idea they were VERY passionate about
- ✔ they **Discovered** what they loved, had a burning desire behind it, including their big WHY
- ✔ they **Designed** a crystal clear "vision" and wrote it down, then read it out loud and often
- ✔ they **Determined** a partner in believing, created a dream team, and defined what their resources were and where they could go for support

The remaining steps toward success are to:

- ✔ **Define** a plan, starting with the end in mind!
- ✔ **Decide on a Deadline** to achieve this goal, and start taking action, even before you feel ready
- ✔ **Dedicate** and never give up. Even when you fail, know this is part of the process. Just dust yourself off, learn from your mistakes, and keep moving
- ✔ **Deliver** a solid money management plan

In keeping with the stepping-stones of these successful kids before you, let's take a look at where you are so far. By now you should feel that your "vision" is clear, have identified a partner in believing and at least one person for your dream team, and have drawn up a list of resources you can tap into.

You also have brought your dream from thought into a written vision and have begun to put this into a written plan of action and to-do list. But wait... I hear that little voice saying, "Hold on here, I'm just a teen!"

Age Requirements

Don't fall into that trap of saying, "I'm not old enough" or "I have to be an adult...to make money or be a financial success." Never ever let fear hold you back from going after what you want. Don't let fears get in the way or stop you in your tracks.

It was Franklin D. Roosevelt who said, "The only thing we have to fear is fear alone." Isn't that the truth!

Age obviously was NOT an obstacle that kept the teens I've already mentioned in this book from achieving their dreams. And in some cases, being a teen can even be an advantage and *help* your success.

Again, if you break it down, the first thing these teens did was to make a decision. Sure, they had a belief that they could do it (or borrowed the belief that someone else had in them) and a strong desire. With these two elements in hand, they made a decision to give it a go and try to make something of their idea.

Without making that decision, the horse is left at the starting gate and can't finish its race (in fact, it can't even make its first bolt in that direction).

"Kids" have been doing amazing things for a long, long time. To prove my point, I looked up some statistics in the *Guinness Book of World Records:*

- ✔ The world's youngest Zumba instructor was only 11
- ✔ The world's youngest kid to hit a hole-in-one in golf was 4
- ✔ The world's youngest stock-broker was only 17
- ✔ The world's youngest X-Games skateboarder was 11
- ✔ The world's youngest club DJ was only 7
- ✔ The world's youngest ice skating world champion was 14
- ✔ The youngest professional drummer was age 4
- ✔ The youngest commercially published female author wrote *"How the World Began"* in 1962, and was only 4
- ✔ Keisha Castle-Hughes was age 13 when nominated for the Best Actress Award for her role in "Whale Rider"

See... age is not an issue, young or old! So never let that hold you back or use it for a lame excuse... ever!

Just keep in mind there are no rules and there are no requirements (especially an age requirement) that will prevent you from following your dreams and being successful. Whether you are 8 or 80, the possibilities and potential are endless.

Mentors and Masters

Speaking of 80, my great-grandmother was a perfect example of somebody stepping into the unknown to try out new things when others think it is impossible.

She was one of my mentors and definitely a master in believing anything is possible if you have a strong enough desire or reason to do it (and are willing to put in the energy and effort to succeed).

Take a look at what my great-grandmother did:

- ✔ went skydiving at age 75
- ✔ started her own micro-lending non profit giving loans to veteran's widows in her 80s
- ✔ wrote a cookbook on food and life, and another book called, *Put a Zip in Your Day* when she was in her 90s

And check this OUT:

- ✔ rode on the back of a Harley-Davison motorcycle 90 miles an hour at age 90!

When I told my friends about what she did later in life, they were like, "No way!"

TIP: It's important to your success to have a mentor who can guide and encourage you along your path to success. Just be careful. Make sure the person you choose to listen to knows what you need to know (or at least has been successful within their own lives).

Lots of people can give advice, but few have actually built a dream! Right now, I could even be considered a mentor to you, as I'm teaching you the path I have followed to being successful.

To find your perfect mentor, look for someone who has done what you want to accomplish. Why try to reinvent the wheel? Go for someone who has done this before. Ask them how they did it. And try to make sure this person shares your same core values as well.

Let's say you want to be a successful skateboarder, but this person does not have the same core values as you do and behaves in a way you are not comfortable with.

Trust me when I say, it will be better in the long run for you to find a new and more suitable mentor.

WARNING: Don't ever listen to someone telling you NOT to go after your dream... especially if they have never gone for theirs!

TREASURE MAP TO SUCCESS

Plan of Attack

"IF YOU WANT TO REACH A GOAL, 'SEE THE REACHING' IN YOUR OWN MIND BEFORE YOU ACTUALLY ARRIVE AT YOUR GOAL."
– ZIG ZIGLAR

I'm 14 and know from personal experience that kids my age want things fast and want them instantly. We are just wired differently than the generations before us. And this is where I keep coming back to "run a mile or a marathon." I choose the mile.

And the fastest way I know to make my own money is to create a plan of attack. Once you have one, then you simply follow it. Like, what is the first thing I'd need? What are the first steps I should take? And so on...

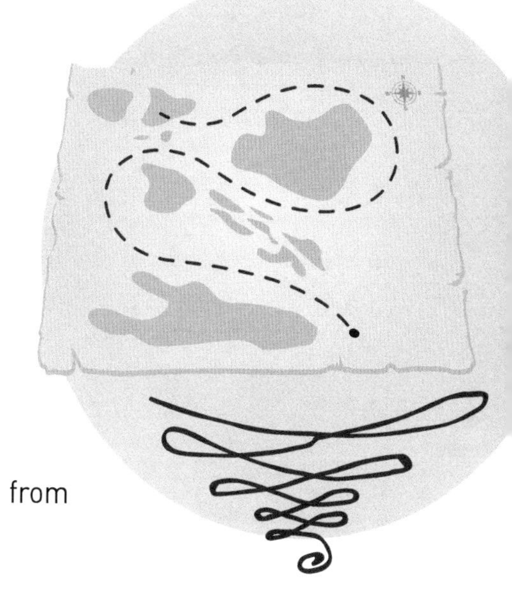

Here is a planning order that works really well:

- ✔ list the things you are good at
- ✔ pick the top 5 (your favorites)
- ✔ then pick 2-3 business ideas from those talents

- ✔ choose the idea with most electricity
- ✔ then reverse engineer that top idea...

Now it's time to combine your money-making ideas, talents, income goals (along with your core values and your positive attitude) and match these up with all the support and resources that are available.

We've come to the part where we create a step-by-step plan of attack to keep focused and on track. Just like when you have a school project.

Everything needs to be put into an A, B, C, planning format. And remember to use that resource list of the people who can help and the materials you have from Chapter 2. All of this will do a world of good for the success of your intended money project or goal.

IDEAS: If you want to sell hair ribbons, you might realize that your little sister's gymnastics team is a perfect place where you could sell them. Or if you want to make cookies and cupcakes and your aunt has a bakery, maybe she could donate some supplies. Or if you want to teach kids soccer, your dad's friend, who is a soccer coach, might have some extra soccer balls.

You see? As I said earlier, you usually have way more resources than you realize. So keep thinking...

TIP: It's way easier to dodge any detours you may find along the way, if you have an ABC plan in advance. And remember, it's less challenging to start with the end in mind and then work backwards.

And I bet by now you're seeing just how important it is to have a sequential step-by-step plan. To anchor this in, let's look at an example of how to make $100 in a few weeks' time by walking dogs:

1. Do a little research and see the # of dogs in my area.
2. Find out if I need a dog-walking license.
3. Gather up the supplies needed to walk dogs, leashes etc. (borrow from friends if I don't have all I need).

4. Go to the local pet store for tips or ideas, and maybe sign up for a dog walking training course.

As you can see, these action steps are very important to take to reach these goals. Again, try to start with the end in mind and work backwards.

I have 11 action items for a dog walking business. If you are literally thinking of starting a small business, you can visit www.MyMomIsNotMyMoney.com to see those and many other resources and step-by-step plans.

SPECIAL NOTE: A point to consider when you begin linking ideas together is that you need to write out every action step sequentially. You can't just jump from "I am creative" to "I can sell poems." Even if the step seems obvious to you, without it, there isn't anything to sell if it's not created yet. Get my point?

GPS Navigation System

Would you agree the most efficient way to get to where you want to go is with a road map (or at least with a good GPS App)? It makes sense, right? So let's do just that... let's create your navigational guide to:

- ✔ have the clear destination in mind (this is your VISION I told you to write)
- ✔ know why you want to go there in the first place (this is your WHY that motivates you to succeed)
- ✔ have a clear step-by-step plan with goals and timelines (this is what you will create next)

Vision

Do you remember when you were little doing those maze puzzles on the back of the kids' menu? When I did them, I would always start from the end and figure my way up to the start.

That way I never got stuck because I was able to identify all the dead-ends and work my way around them. You should do the same.

EXAMPLE: I would like to take my love of cooking to make cupcakes and cookies and sell them door to door and make $100 bucks. And I would like to keep $80 for myself and donate $20 to buy gifts for the families in need that my church is supporting this Christmas. So what steps would I need to take?

Well, here is my plan of attack for that:

- ✔ I create a "vision" or "blueprint" of the result I want and the deadline for when I want to accomplish this goal.
- ✔ I set my money goal at $100 and decide to donate $20.
- ✔ I plan on starting this coming weekend.
- ✔ I plan on selling soccer cookies and cupcakes at the local soccer tournament at halftime two weeks away.
- ✔ Find a friend to agree to be on my D.R.E.A.M. Team.
- ✔ Ask my aunt who has a bakery if I can use her kitchen.
- ✔ I mark on my calendar that I'm going to bake on the night before the soccer game.
- ✔ I mark on my calendar buying the supplies I need the week before.
- ✔ I mark my calendar to take 20% of the money earned to my church on the Monday after the soccer tournament.

Now it's your turn. Take a moment right now to write out in reverse order your A, B, C plan of action. Create it similar to the example above that has specific action steps you can take to reach your goals, and include the support of your D.R.E.A.M. Team.

EXAMPLE: A step-by-step sequence for writing this book would begin like this... *the first thing I will do is make an outline of what the book will cover. The next thing I will do is pre-sell the book to cover my costs to produce it. The next thing I will do is..."*

Timelines and Decisions

A big part of reaching your money goal is to see the life you want to live, now, six months from now, a year from now by visualizing it in your mind in advance. These are milestones and goals.

Just like rungs of a ladder help you reach the roof of your house and take you places higher than your own two feet can, goals with timelines and deadlines added to them have much more power and substance.

Different goals match different dreams. There are easy short-term goals. And there are long-term and larger ones that might take more time to achieve.

For example, a goal where I want $40 bucks to go out and buy a new pair of jeans by next weekend, this is a shorter-term smaller idea... one that can be whipped out like boom, boom, boom.

Begin to think of other ideas like: I can have a garage sale, lemonade stand, or bake some cookies to make some fast cash. Or maybe it's a longer-term dream that takes multiple steps to achieve with bigger rewards.

Either way, you need to set your goals with the end in mind, and then make a decision to go out and do it, followed with a solid plan to support that idea.

SPECIAL NOTE: There is an order to the list of things required. Support is on the list, but it's not the first. Decision comes before support. You could have all the support in the world, like "Allie you can do this, Allie you can do this..." but it's not just a matter of support. You have to want to take action. And it all starts with deciding that..."I'm gonna do this thing."

Case in point, why do you think the kids I've used as examples within this book were able to achieve their success? It's in part because they were not willing to be stopped by conditions as they were, and most importantly, they made a decision to do it.

There is a critical point where you say, "I'm going to be the person who generates my own money." To illustrate my point, take a look at the people who sit around "thinking" about being a person who generates their own money, and who talk to lots of people about it, but never end up becoming one. Why is that?

The answer is easy...they never make the *decision to be that person.* Don't be one of those people. Or you might get left at the starting gate of your own race.

DISEMPOWER THE FEAR

Did you know, just like many other things, imagination can be looked at as being a double-edged sword. Huh?

That's right, even though imagination can be such an amazing tool in creating ways to improve your life and accomplish your goals, on the flipside, it can cause havoc and create chaos as well.

Really? Well, let's take a closer look at this.

Your memory can be used for both directions. Yes, memory certainly looks towards the past. But don't only think of what's in the past, you can use it for the future too. Like in two directions.

Think of it this way, you can use it to create a really scary life for yourself, or you can use it to open doors and empower you. It's a huge power resource, but we misuse its true gifts when we scare ourselves with it.

IMAGINATION + TWO DIRECTIONS

Fear and Focus Gone Wild

> "YOU BLOCK YOUR DREAM WHEN YOU ALLOW OUR FEAR TO GROW BIGGER THAN YOUR FAITH"
> – MARY MORRISSEY

Everybody has an imagination and it works perfectly when used to create things. Yet some people choose to use it for fear, and in doing so, focus its power in only one direction.

How often have you watched a scary movie and that night, or the next, you were afraid to go anywhere? Sure, you might not have admitted it to others, but you didn't even have the courage to get up and walk the long dark hallway to the bathroom!

Creatures in the Closet

That's when imagination goes to the dark side. Even though pop star Kelly Clarkson sings about loving your dark side, we don't need to let the dark sides of our imagination hold us back.

It's like after watching a scary movie. It's been proven that if you stare blindly in the dark, you start creating all kinds of horrible stuff in your mind, aka a floating balloon that suddenly turns into a hovering ghost.

Take this concept into your money-making and business activities. What happens when it comes time to sell your ideas or products? Don't start imagining everyone turning you down. That's not going to get you anywhere, other than going in the wrong direction. And, perhaps down a one-way street to nowhere fast.

Like I said, if you stare somewhere for awhile in the dark, your mind starts putting together a figure of some sort. There you are lying in your bed afraid to get out and run for the door, because something underneath will surely grab your legs. Right?

Then while you are trying to figure out what to do, you start seeing all sorts of things moving just behind your clothes (because you happened to leave the closet door open). Oh no, what are you going to do now? Hold your breath and hope someone comes to save you... that's it!

What if you started doing that with your business ideas? If you let your imagination go the opposite direction of being successful, you're going to run into trouble. You're going to let your mind stop you dead in your tracks. And most likely even before you really get started. What a shame that would be...

Floating Ideas and Memory

Have you ever had a great idea come to you while you were dreaming? Yes, we all have most likely. But who can ever remember them once you get up and get on with your day?

Dreams are just floating ideas that drift in and out of our minds. They are there for a fleeting moment and then, poof. They are gone. The trick is to do your best to capture them when they come. That way, they can't just slip away without a trace.

What about memory? Let's go back to the subject of memory. Have you ever heard a song on the radio (or someone's phone/iPod) and try to remember it without writing it down? And when you get home and try really hard to remember the name or any part of the lyrics, they are gone?

The good news is that eventually the Internet saves you, after a quick search. But what you have is not a lack of memory because we are born with a perfect memory. It's really just a lack of recall.

Like I said, our memory can be used in two directions. It can be used to see things from the past, and it can be used to fuel the future when combined with the power of our imagination.

The trick is to use the experiences we or others have had from the past with our creative powers to enhance and improve on those ideas.

You see, creative thought is just that. It has the power to create just about anything. Think of Walt Disney for example. Out of his imagination came a fantasy world called Disneyland. And from that initial idea, came a entire world of new ideas, with characters, movies, amusement parks, and so much more.

Each of our thoughts are things. They have a magnetic pull and this is scientifically proven just like gravity. And, by focusing on positive things, we literally create a magnetic pull to bring what we want to us.

The section titled "thoughts become things" (Chapter 1) was inspired by the whole scientific objects idea. If you put enough positive stuff on and around an object, then other positive things are naturally attracted to it like a magnet. They automatically get pulled towards it. In other words... quantum physics.

We all have the power to project our visions of the future and let the magnetic pull line it up perfectly. Which is why I asked you to write down your vision and make up your own vision board. By doing these things, you are using your imagination to create a future memory.

That's when you are using the power of memory in two directions... and to your benefit. The more often you do this, the easier it is, and the more powerful it also becomes. Really, I promise.

MAKING FORWARD PROGRESS

Take the Steps You Can

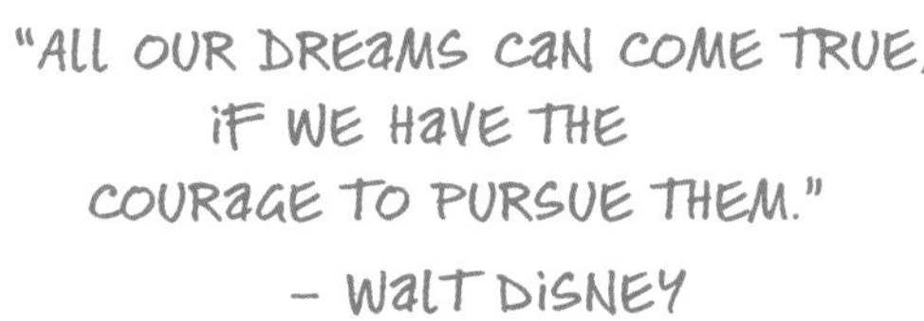

I've talked before about taking the steps that you can with what you already have. And maybe you don't completely know what I mean by that or how to actually do that for yourself.

So what I want to do now is address those things that will either get you stuck (and stop you in your tracks without taking any steps forward) or will be the very reason you keep going until you reach success.

I Don't Know How

One of the biggest roadblocks is the "I don't know how" syndrome. "How do I do that?" "How am I going to do something like that?" "How can I do that without any money?" And the list goes on and on...

A great way to start getting better ideas is by asking better questions. Instead of beginning your list of 20 ideas with "how" can I make $100 bucks by this coming Saturday...start your list by asking a question this way instead:

"What could I do that would provide someone great value and in exchange for that service I will receive $100.00 for my efforts?"

Doesn't this feel like it's lighter and has more energy and life? By tying in the part about how you will positively affect someone or something by your efforts, you will receive better ideas. It just works that way. The "how" questions feel a lot less empowering and almost as if you are just out to "get" something.

Once you begin to ask better questions, you will be able to receive better answers. The better your answers become, the more obvious the "how" is, which makes it almost second nature to "know" how to do whatever it is you need to do.

Decide On a Deadline... Like Now

When are you going to get started and take action? Now is as good a time as any! Begin by marking on your calendar the deadlines for your money-making goals and when you will start taking your first action step (outlined in the plan of attack you created earlier in this chapter).

Most kids wait and put it off. That's normal. But, will this get you making any money? This is the attitude of people who never succeed. They never feel ready.

Let me tell you something... if I'd waited until I felt ready, this book wouldn't be in your hands right now. If President Kennedy waited until they had every answer, we never would have walked on the moon.

TIP: This is your moment. Decide to take action, even though you might not feel ready. You can start where you are with what you have.

Just take the first step, even if you don't know what the next step is yet. That's okay, once you take the first step, often the next step appears.

Remember the actor Harrison Ford in "Indiana Jones and the Last Crusade?" There was a moment in that movie where Indiana Jones comes to a cliff knowing he needs to get to the other side.

He couldn't "see" the bridge, but has to take a step into thin air knowing he could fall to his death. After he takes the first step, an invisible bridge begins to appear below his feet. More appears with each step.

This often happens in life, but the trick is to just take that first step. I did this when I decided to pre-sell this book even before I had an outline or before any of the pages were written.

All I had was the idea, the name, and a basic concept.

But I knew if I took the first step and pre-sold the book, it would motivate me actually to finish it. And you know what? It did...

End of Chapter Recap:

Now is the time for you to create your own "Plan" of action... if you haven't already. Use some blank paper and write down all of your ideas. You can even create your own business-building folder where you can put in your written vision, your list of resources, and now add to it your action plan.

Make sure your plan includes:

- ✔ a clear destination (refer to your "vision")
- ✔ "why" you want to go there in the first place (and what motivates you to succeed)
- ✔ a clear step-by-step plan with goals and timelines (this is your GPS guide and roadmap)

BONUS POINTS: Take a moment now. Sit back, relax, and in your mind, play the movie of you living out your dreams and accomplishing what you have written in your vision. You do this at least once per day. As you do this, think about your WHY and your deep burning desire! Is it to be free of having to ask your parents for money and feeling confident in your own talents? Is it to help others in need? To give something special to a family member? Get in touch, once again, with your burning desire right now... and really feel what your life will be like once you have it.

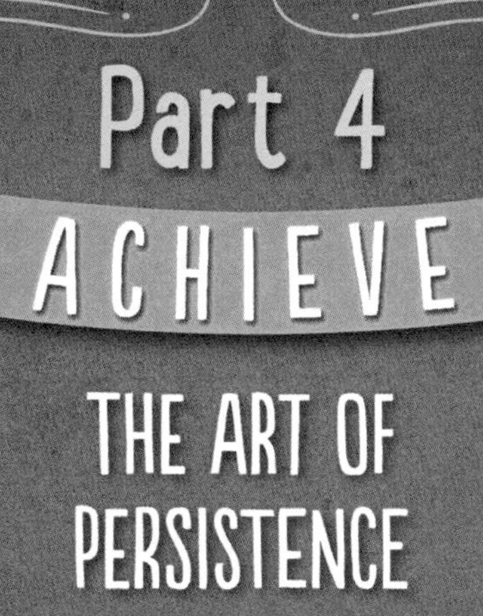

Part 4
ACHIEVE
THE ART OF PERSISTENCE

"A Crow, half-dead with thirst, came upon a Pitcher which had once been full of water; but when the Crow put its beak into the mouth of the Pitcher he found that only very little water was left in it, and that he could not reach far enough down to get at it. He tried, and he tried, but at last had to give up in despair. Then a thought came to him, and he took a pebble and dropped it into the Pitcher. Then he took another pebble and dropped that into the Pitcher. Then he took another pebble and dropped that into the Pitcher. Then he took another pebble and dropped that into the Pitcher. Then he took another pebble and dropped that into the Pitcher. Then he took another pebble and dropped that into the Pitcher. At last, at last, he saw the water mount up near him, and after casting in a few more pebbles he was able to quench his thirst and save his life."

– The Crow and the Pitcher

THE ART OF PERSISTENCE

In This Chapter

- ✔ Seeing how failure can be a good thing despite what others think
- ✔ Taking a look at bold actions and thinking big
- ✔ Looking at drive and determination and working the dream

"IF YOU LEARN FROM DEFEAT, YOU HAVEN'T REALLY LOST."
– ZIG ZIGLAR

The lesson to Aesop's fable "The Fox Without a Tail" is to see that whether it's one pebble or one dollar at a time, big goals are often accomplished little by little.

Even though it may take awhile, you will accomplish your goals with steady persistence, particularly if you are highly motivated by drive or necessity. In other words, if we take one step each day towards our goals with whatever we have, we will make progress. That is a given and an example of determination.

In this chapter, we will explore both failure and how what others think can mistakenly guide your actions. We will look at how shifting from negative to positive can improve your chances of success and how it can also enhance the lives of others around you. Remember, motivation and determination are the fuel that will keep you from ever giving up too soon.

DELETE DEFEAT

Be honest, haven't you been taught to never surrender, and to not entertain the subject of defeat? Well I am here to tell you that defeat isn't the end of the world. Even the most successful people in the world have had a taste of it at one time or another.

Just like a computer gives you the option to hit the "delete" button, I'd like you to delete some of your beliefs about defeat. And that begins with a big one, worrying about what your friends, family, or others think if you attempt something and do not succeed.

For a moment, I'd like to you borrow my belief that losing is not always a bad thing.

WHAT WILL OTHERS THINK?

Be Yourself

"A PERSON WHO NEVER MADE A MISTAKE NEVER TRIED ANYTHING NEW."
– ALBERT EINSTEIN

When you're not afraid to lose, you can just play. When you don't care what other people think, you can just be yourself. Have you ever felt like you have been held back by society's opinion that nobody is good enough? Well, don't let other people's limitations glue you to security. Don't be afraid of being great at something, and standing out.

People like our family or friends may tell us that it's okay to stand out, to be "the daisy out of a field of plain blades of grass." Yet we neglect to pay attention to their feedback and discount it, having programmed in our minds that, "They are *supposed* to say that because they love us." Like being on remote control.

We hear this advice, but we sometimes don't really listen to the true message in it. If you look closely, all successful people have a great amount of self-confidence and self-esteem. Not only do they stand out in a crowd, but they are not afraid to make an error or a mistake. They simply go for it.

And when they do inevitably fail, they get back up, dust themselves off, and get right back in the game. That's why they're a success, and not at home crying about their past failures.

Heads or Tails

Let's take another look from the other side of the coin. We all know a quarter has two sides, heads and tails. And just like in the game, "head or tails," we see that one side is for the winner and the other is the loser.

Such is life. There's that negative side to everything around us, and there is the flip side, which is positive.

I believe a positive can be found in anything. It's just a matter of what you choose to see, the positive or the negative? So let me ask you this; which makes you feel more alive? Looking at a glass half empty, or half full? Guess what... if life gives you lemons, *you* get to choose to make lemonade or not:

- ✔ You have the power to see the glass half full.
- ✔ You have the power to shift your attitude.
- ✔ You have the power to see the best in others and yourself.
- ✔ You have the power to make someone feel good with your words or actions.

This is a positive force you might not even be aware of, but just know it's always within you and available at all times. Choose how you want to look at it.

Re-Boot With a Platinum Upgrade

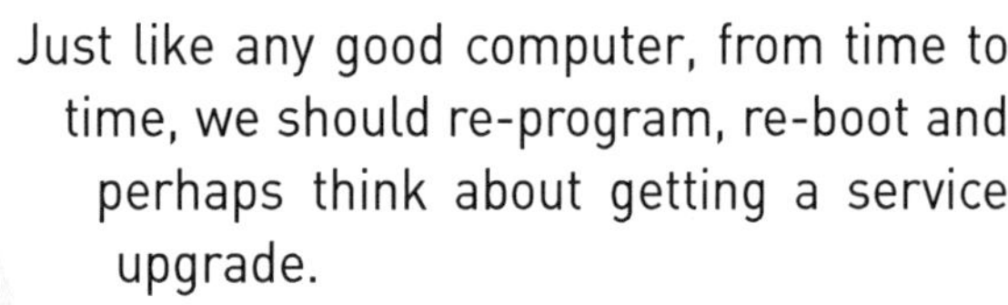

Just like any good computer, from time to time, we should re-program, re-boot and perhaps think about getting a service upgrade.

Things are changing fast and it can be hard to keep up when technology is advancing so quickly. So let's take a minute to hit the refresh button and clear the outdated data from our thinking patterns.

For example, when we try to compare ourselves to others or other things, most of the time that means something and/or someone is up or down, good or bad, better or worse. That is the data in our thinking patterns.

A better way to look at this is when we begin to compare ourselves to another person, it's more about you being at your best and being the best that you can be.

This to me is the best type of upgrade in your way of thinking and in your perspective. Concentrating on being a better "you" is where your focus should be, without getting caught up trying to be as good as or better than someone else.

Speaking of perspective, there is a scene in the movie, *Bridge to Taribithia* with Josh Hutchison, where he and his friend go and explore the woods to find a place of their own. They climb a tree and look over the land and she says, "Wow can you believe this is all ours and we are the rulers of all this beautiful land?"

He looks at her like she is crazy and says "I don't see anything!" The camera's point of view changes and instead of the amazing land we saw moments before with vibrant colors and waterfalls, now all we see is just a plain, dried up valley. Josh's character says, "I don't get it, what do you see?"

And she says, "Just close your eyes, but keep your mind wide open and use your imagination." He tries once but it doesn't work, so she tells him to try again. He takes a deep breath, tries again and opens his eyes. All of a sudden, he sees this beautiful land before him, and their eyes meet when she says, "It's called Tarabithia!"

That is the power of changing your perspective...

FAILURE CAN BE A GOOD THING

Not Afraid to Lose

"IN ORDER TO SUCCEED, YOUR DESIRE FOR SUCCESS SHOULD BE GREATER THAN YOUR FEAR OF FAILURE."
– BILL COSBY

Here we are again, back to that "failure" thing that makes most of us afraid or uncomfortable. Remember how I said there have been zillions of successful people who have also experienced failure and defeat? Well, let's take a closer look into that with a few case studies or examples.

The quicker I can show you that failing at something does not mean you are a failure, the sooner you will be on your way to achieving your dreams and being successful more often than not.

For example, you know the famous hop-hop dancer, "Twitch" from "So You Think You Can Dance?" When he tried out for the show, he didn't make the cut the first time he auditioned. Actually, it took him four years until he finally made the show. That's four years in a row, he auditioned and failed!

Most people would have given up after the second or third year, you know? But he didn't. And now he's one of the most popular hip-hop dancers in the world.

He was even featured in the hip-hop "Step-Up" movies. This is a perfect story of what total drive and unending determination looks like... and can do for us. Twitch didn't let initial defeat keep him from his dreams, and look at him now!

Wins and Losses

How about Abraham Lincoln? I bet you didn't know about all his "failures?" Now there is a pretty amazing example of someone never losing sight of what they really wanted to do. His path was certainly not paved in gold, and he had setbacks and defeats all along the way. But he became our 16th President. Abraham Lincoln is one of the greatest examples of persistence and someone who did not quit and learned from his setback and failures.

- ✔ he was born into poverty
- ✔ he lost eight elections
- ✔ he failed in business at least twice
- ✔ he suffered a nervous breakdown...

If anyone had cause to quit, it was Lincoln. But he didn't quit... and after much drive, determination, inner strength and commitment, he became one of the greatest presidents in U.S. history. Unlike most, Lincoln did not let any of these challenges, including personal and business bankruptcy, discourage him from going after his dreams. He persisted and did not let the "so-called" failures bring him down.

Some might have given up after losing those elections. Others might have given up after suffering such personal loss and multiple bankruptcies. But then there are those who know that mistakes and challenges make us stronger. It's people who believe and think like this who become the leaders and true examples of success.

Learning From Our Mistakes

What if you try and fail? No problem. Think of it as the gift of feedback. It's valuable information that can help redirect you to something that's much better for you in the long run.

My grandmother says, "Failure is not a step back or an obstacle, it is a learning opportunity that will help you determine your path to building your dream."

So if this is true, maybe we can turn a failure into a learning opportunity that considers the reasons why you got stuck or did not succeed. Some good questions to ask yourself are:

- ✔ How can I see this differently?
- ✔ What ideas could I use from this experience?
- ✔ What new ideas might make a difference here?
- ✔ Who might be able to help turn this around?
- ✔ **What other possible solutions are there other than giving up on my dream?**

You can fail nine times, but it may be that tenth idea where you succeed. Never give in to the failure.

Persistence

DEDICATE AND DELIVER

What does it mean to fully dedicate yourself to going after and achieving your dreams, desires, or goals? Does it mean having a casual interest or so-so drive to have something or another? Or does it take more than that to accomplish your goals?

These are some of the things that need to be addressed when it comes to your "money-making" success.

By practicing positive persistence and through real dedication, you will be successful – guaranteed!

So let's take a quick peek at some of the things you need to do and other things you may want to avoid on your path towards making your own money. Let's steer clear of anything that could hold you back.

For, example, if you are going door-to-door selling cupcakes, you don't want to imagine the worst and let your fear of everyone saying no get in your way. You have to switch the channel to one that imagines everyone buying all of your cupcakes as soon as you make them so you are successful.

FACE YOUR FEARS

Take Bold Action

> "IT WAS CHARACTER THAT GOT US OUT OF BED, COMMITMENT THAT MOVED US INTO ACTION AND DISCIPLINE THAT ENABLED US TO FOLLOW THROUGH."
> – ZIG ZIGLAR

In order to achieve our goals and dreams, we must be willing to face our fears. These fear busters include things like, not caring what others will say or think, taking action and risking failure.

Here are three very important tips to remember:

- ✔ Face your fear, and take big bold action each day.
- ✔ Even when you fail or make a mistake, keep your head up and keep moving towards your dream with inspired initiative each day.
- ✔ Never give up, even when you fail, dust yourself off, learn from your mistakes, and keep moving in the direction of your dreams!

For practice, write down a few bold actions you can take today that face your fears and will move you in the direction of your dreams. As soon as you take that first action, it's time to take the next big bold action and then, the next.

Each day you should be taking at least one baby step, and some days big, bold steps, towards your goals.

Person of Increase

My little brothers had an exercise in school this year where they were learning about being either a "bucket filler" or a "bucket dipper." This might sound weird, but it's kind of a good analogy.

Let's say when you say something nice or give a compliment to someone... you fill up their bucket. If instead, you say a put-down, or post a mean comment online, then you are actually being a bucket dipper.

So successful people are people who think of ways to be nice, kind, and brighten up another's day. They don't engage in gossip, or bullying, or put-downs.

TIP: Be a positive person of increase and a bucket filler. In doing so, you will see way more success in your life as opposed to residing in the negative.

Garbage In – Garbage Out

A lot of what I am saying in this book revolves around the way we think and use our mind. I have said before that we need to be careful what we allow into our mind and who we invite to share in our dreams, goals and aspirations.

Well the same is to be said for where our focus lies. How much time do you spend watching stupid TV shows or YouTube videos? I'm not saying to never do that, because let me tell you I love Jacks Gap, Marcus Butler,

Casper Lee... I mean I can go on forever. But what I'm saying here is to pay attention to what you are paying attention to:

- ✔ do you watch reality (or "unreality") shows?
- ✔ how much mindless gossip do you entertain?
- ✔ what kind of books do you read?
- ✔ are your friends positive and supportive, or do they gossip about others?

It's important to know what sort of stuff is going into your brain and even better to understand how those things get filtered and spit back out. Plus the saying, "What goes around comes around" is really true.

If you say mean things about others, if you gossip, it's putting negative energy out into the world. If you lie, cheat, or steal, this puts negative energy into the world. And the opposite is also true. If you say nice things to help uplift someone's spirit and you are an honest giving person, you are putting positive energy out into the world. Whatever you put out, it WILL come back to you ten times over.

EXERCISE: Write down ways that you were nice and caring to someone you know, and ways that you told the truth and did the right thing. Notice how you feel when you write about the good things you've done? Now go ahead and write a positive commitment to yourself that goes like this:

"I am a positive person, I tell the truth, I work hard and at all times, I show myself and others love and kindness."

THINK BIG

Glued to Security

"DON'T LET OTHERS WITH SMALL MINDS LIMIT YOUR DREAMS, THEY MIGHT SEE IT AS BIG BUT OTHERS WITH BIG MINDS MAY SEE IT AS SMALL."

–ALLIE JOY

When I said at the beginning of this chapter, "Don't let other people's limitations glue you to security," what I meant by that is pretty much summed up in a quote by Steve Jobs:

"Here's to the crazy ones, the misfits, the rebels, the troublemakers, the round pegs in the square holes... the ones who see things differently — they're not fond of rules... You can quote them, disagree with them, glorify or vilify them, but the only thing you can't do is ignore them because they change things... they push the human race forward, and while some may see them as the crazy ones, we see genius, because the ones who are crazy enough to think that they can change the world, are the ones who do."

In other words, dare to be you. Dare to dream big. Dare to be unique. Be bold and watch your success rise over and over again for being brave enough to break free from the mold of society and be different.

Have you ever been in a situation when you allow yourself to be vulnerable and share some of your ideas or creative genius? But the second that it slips out of your lips, someone around you shoves it down and trashes it. Like when I was talking to my friend about getting a custom car and she said it was too expensive.

Without even trying, she dismissed the idea as crazy. Those were her limitations speaking. Or like I said before, those are pre-programmed paradigms which limit her from accepting the idea that she is able to get whatever she wants. Deliberately looking into her future, she planted the thought of not having enough money, so she would have to get a summer job and save penny by penny for a used car.

My friend didn't even go as far as a new car, she even limited that minor detail. She glued herself to security. Now I agree it's normal to go along with your peers because you don't want to be the lone ranger. And I have been in that position, sitting around at sleepovers looking into the future and every one around me is thinking into a "normal" American life. The expected.

But, I'm going to encourage you to NOT be afraid to think big. If everyone else is living in a small bubble, it doesn't mean you have to do that too. You are young, you can explore, and build your own life. Be unique, that's way more fun!

Steve Jobs also said, *"When you grow up you tend to be told that the world is the way that it is and your job is to live your life inside the world and try not to get in trouble and maybe get an education and make some money and have a family."*

And never compare yourself to others. Remember this is one of the Golden Rules; there will always be someone better than you, and you will be better than some. So, remain humble and be grateful... these are the qualities that no one can take away from you.

Ashton Kutcher says, *"Everything we call life was made up of people that are no smarter than you. And you can build your own things and you can build your own life that other people can live in. So build a life, don't live one, find your opportunities and always be thoughtful, generous, and most of all, kind."*

Don't Settle

The last thing you want to do when you are going after your dreams and goals is to settle for less. That's what so many people seem to do. Settle. They say things like, "I really want that (fill in the blanks), but there's no way to get it. Or, they say, "I will make do with this (fill in the blanks)." How sad is that?

We were not put on this planet to just survive. We came here to survive and live fully. So why would we want to settle for less? I just don't get it. This doesn't make any sense to me.

To anchor in that point, here's another great quote from Steve Jobs: *"Your work is going to fill a large part of your life, and the only way to be truly satisfied is to do what you believe is great work. And the only way to do great work is to love what you do. If you haven't found it yet, keep looking. Don't settle. As with all matters of the heart, you'll know when you find it."*

Not only should you not settle for less, but you should also be focused and determined. If you have a strong desire, do whatever you can to make it happen.

For example, take a look at an experience that my Uncle Rich had when he was in high school. He thought he needed money to rent a tuxedo for his upcoming prom. The obvious thing and only way he could think of to get the tuxedo was to pay $80 for the rental.

So, in earnest he asked my Grandma for the money. She said that he didn't really need $80, he needed a tuxedo. At first, he was confused.

She then asked him what were the steps he would take if he did have the money.

My uncle said, if he had the money, then he would go down to the store and try on tuxedos to find the one he wanted and reserve it. My Grandma suggested he go ahead and do that even though he did not see how he was going to pay for it.

Even though he thought is was a waste of time, and he felt a little silly going, that's what he actually did. And while he was at the store, the manager asked him what school he went to, and my uncle told him HilHi.

Little did Uncle Rich know, but that tuxedo store was having high school students in the area wear one of their tuxedos to their schools every Friday for the month leading up until prom. This was their way of showcasing their tuxedos to the kids so they'd be interested in coming to their store to rent.

And what do you think ended up happening? The store employee offered my uncle the opportunity to be his school's representative, and in exchange for that, he got a free tuxedo to wear to prom! No $80 required!

Isn't that a great story? So think for a minute... what do you want right now that you "think" you can't have because you don't have the money? Now, what if there was a way to get it that didn't require actual cash? Good question right?

All Work and No Play

When most people start looking at starting their own businesses, they just see work. No fun. But when you are doing what you love, you actually have fun. And even when it's hard work, that's part of the joys in life.

I know of this girl who enjoyed playing with lotion and perfumes. After a while, she realized that she was passionate about inventing these types of products, mixing them, and making her own potions.

She then went to her mom and they researched how to make their own beauty products. And you know what? Her business of all natural body products are now sold in Nordstrom's!

What she did was take what interested her and decided to create something fun out of it. WOW, this can be you! Well, maybe you don't care about lotions or perfumes, but the point remains, any one of us can make money doing something we are interested in if we really put ourselves into it.

So, if you are looking to make a little extra money (or want to start a big business idea), it isn't really that hard. Just find something that you really enjoy, and that you are already doing, then find a place to start beginning with what you have.

To illustrate my point, let's say you love basketball. Well, you can create your own kind of ball. Or you can create your own mini-basketball camp. Just get together with a friend if you want, create some flyers, go out to your neighborhood park and play some ball. Literally just pick something you enjoy.

REMEMBER: How I said you could play with little kids and get paid for it? Well expand on that idea and see where it takes you. How do you think the first jolly jump or day-care center ideas came from? It was more than likely from someone who really enjoyed playing themselves and took their idea and expanded on it.

DRIVE WITH DETERMINATION

When your friends or parents don't like something you are doing or approve of your ideas, then this shouldn't affect you, it's just their opinion (unless of course you *really* are doing something dumb or stupid...lol).

So even though everyone has a right to their own opinions, they shouldn't pull you down in the process. That is as long as what you are doing is aligned with your core values, and you aren't going directly against your parent's wishes (lol). Just make sure you aren't following someone else's dream.

Follow your heart to your own dreams! While everyone has a right to their own opinions, they shouldn't pull you down in the process.

Again, this comes down to things like self-esteem and confidence. If you are relying on what other people think of you or your ideas, you just may be heading down a road towards disappointing results. I'm not saying you should never seek out the opinions of others, I'm just saying don't accept their "no's" as yours.

Katie Perry is a good example of this. Her parents didn't want her to be a pop singer in Hollywood, but she decided to listen to her heart and go after her dream anyway. She worked very hard. She failed many times trying to make it.

Many people in Hollywood told her that she wouldn't make it. They tried to make her something she wasn't. And then she found a partner in believing, stayed with who she knew she was, committed to her core values, and yes, she finally succeeded. And in a big way!

FROM REALISTIC TO OPTIMISTIC

Drive and Motivation

"ENERGY IS CONTAGIOUS. IT CAN BRING YOU DOWN OR LIFT YOU UP. CHOOSE TO BE AROUND POSITIVE ENERGY DAILY AND YOU WILL BECOME A FLAME FOR OTHERS TO CATCH FIRE WITH."
– DAVE AUSTIN

What you really need to do to be successful, is to stay positive and keep your attention and imagination running in the right direction. And in case you were wondering, that's in the forward moving direction.

Again, think of it as jet fuel. What good is a private Lear Jet if it doesn't have the proper fuel to get up off the ground? No good at all. You'd be better off using your bike to get you where you want to go. It's a lot lighter to get moving at least.

EXAMPLE: Let's take a look at just a simple thing like words. Instead of saying, "if" I succeed, say "when" I succeed. That way, it's a much more powerful thought.

And even if we just let life handle the things we don't know how to do, or aren't quite clear about yet, we can still be successful. Like my Uncle Rich, going to the store to try on tuxedos even though he didn't know how to get one. This is a great example of going for your dream, one step at a time.

But we will need to put in all the effort we can, and give it our best by taking little steps first. Keep that up and those little steps will soon grow into one big monster leap of success.

Positive Energy and Optimism

When I said before that you have the power to make your idea run a mile or run a marathon, I meant that you don't have to keep your ideas to just that one thing in order to take it to the top. You can have more than one and do them at the same time. And with positive energy, you can begin building positive momentum.

For example, a girl named Jill at 17 made belt buckles and sold band concert pictures. This is when eBay was new and belt buckles were big. She went downtown and bought supplies to make them, and then she noticed that even the normal ones being sold in stores were super expensive. So, she sold hers online for a really good price. And made tons of her own cash.

Then she went to a concert, took some photos and sold those online too. Her motivation was to live on her college campus and get enough money to support herself. Every day she would envision herself on the college campus and she talked about it every day. And do you know what happened? Just with belt buckles and photos alone, she made $10,000.00.

Isn't that cool?

From being a teen who thinks in "realistic terms," we can expand into being an "optimistic teen," and it doesn't even have to take more than a split-second for this to occur. In imagining your dreams, you don't want to be too rigid and only reach for the things you know are within your reach or possible.

Put some spice in your visions by remaining optimistic and keeping your expectations high. Do you think those kids who went chasing after Sir Richard Branson were stuck in "being" realistic. I know a bunch of adults who would love to meet that guy, heck I would too, but these two kids had an idea and took action when an opportunity presented itself.

Think for a moment, what can you do today with what you have? Business coach and personal development expert, Bob Proctor, says that the cardinal principle of decision-making is, *"Decide right where you are with whatever you've got. You don't need to know how."*

Whether you think you can or can't...doesn't really matter (unless you let that stop you from trying). Don't allow your reasons, excuses, or circumstances get in your way. Tattoo that into your mind (and you don't even need parental permission for that tattoo...lol).

Once you agree to the possibility and decide with dedication to it, trust me, the rest will all work out. The only thing you have to do is make little steps that get you closer to your goal. It's that simple.

What little step can you take TODAY (right now) towards your money-making goal? Can you call a friend to help? Make a cool flyer? Bake some cookies? Do an extra chore for your mom or dad for extra cash?

Hey, I'm not kidding. Get up and go do something right now...this book will be here when you get back!

TIP: If you want some pre-designed flyers for your business, go to www.MyMomIsNotMyMoney.com and download some cool stuff I've created to help you promote your business.

Quantum Leaps

And you can see in Jill's belt buckle example, she kept it simple and took every step she could. She went downtown, invested a little on supplies, took a few photos at a concert, and then just put them all up on eBay... then boom! She had $10,000 bucks in earnings.

Now, she didn't make it become a huge business that she had to run forever. She had a single goal, she came up with her idea, she took solid action, duplicated her idea with a second variation, and she made it happen.

But then later on at age 21, because she had built up a confidence in herself, she started a brand new business of inspiring teens and giving them self-confidence as a motivational speaker and author. That's an example of a "quantum leap."

Another example is one kid at age 12 who created an app called Bubble-Ball. This one idea has already made over $1 million, and all he did was go find out how to actually make the app, and then created it out of his own imagination.

He put it up on the Apple Store and before he knew it, it was number one passing right by Angry Birds! Like Jill, he also did every step he could take. He came up with an idea, went to the library and researched technology, and then invested some time to put it up for sale. It is now making him money in his sleep and every day he profits from that one idea alone.

NEVER GIVING UP

Work the Dream

"DON'T GIVE UP ON YOUR DREAMS,
OR YOUR DREAMS
WILL GIVE UP ON YOU."
– JOHN WOODEN

I was very inspired by a story of a woman my Grandma coached, who wanted to open up her own restaurant. In order to do this, she needed a loan from the bank and went to a total of 21 banks, but they all said no. It had almost been a year of negotiating and pleading, and still every one of them kept turning her down and slamming doors in her face.

Yet, she had persistence. It was her dream to own her own restaurant and she had already made a decision, in her mind, how it would look, etc. She then asked another bank and once again they still said no.

At this point she was on the edge of giving up when she thought, "well, I didn't have it anyways, so there's nothing to lose. I'll just keep asking until someone says yes." I don't know about you, but I think most people would give up at this point. But she didn't, and at last, the 23rd bank she went to finally said yes. She opened her restaurant and within a couple of weeks, the line was literally out the door and around the block.

If you want to be the person who makes your own money and is successful at reaching your goals and dreams, you will need to work hard and never give up. Trust me, some days you will feel tired, and you just won't want to work at your dream.

There are times you might just want to lay on the couch and watch

TV. But that is not going to get you to your dream, is it? In order to be successful, you must decide now to work harder than you may feel like doing. I'm not saying you can't keep a balance and have fun too. But I just don't want you to give up on your dream too soon, okay?

Here's a secret that will really help. Don't let your lazy side win the war. You know the feeling when you procrastinate doing work, homework or studying? Well, the next thing you know, you have to cram it in before class and/or forget to even do it at all. You then most likely get a bad grade.

And the whole reason you do it is for the good grade and approval, right? That is your why. The reason you actually ripped yourself off the couch and opened the textbook in the first place?

Well, we all have that voice that is like a rope pulling us back. That also goes back to the reason you have your big why. It's the other side of the scale, and plays tug-o-war with your positive and negative sides.

Just muster up enough persistence to pull it over the line to win. Even though it takes energy and time, believe me it's definitely worth it. And before you know it you will be looking at your big shiny trophy.

Set for Purpose

As a reminder, once you have your vision, make sure you set a purpose and plan how much money you want to have once your vision comes to life. It is not enough to just say, I want a lot of money. You have to write down the exact amount, and then write down a date.

Put a due date on it, put that onto your calendar, and then get working towards that.

If you aren't specific and you don't actually put some real intentions behind it, you will just end up procrastinating and let your reasons get in the way.

EXAMPLE: With my book, I first decided to begin writing the chapters. Little by little, my book started to form. I then thought, how can I make money now, so I had the idea to pre-sell my book. Without the chapters even being done yet, but I put a due date on it and put it on the calendar.

By doing this, it created a REAL feeling of the book being done in my mind, and I also needed to fulfill my commitment to sending the book out to those people who trusted me and pre-bought the book. How's that for a "no turning back" rule?

Just take every step you can take today and each and every day. Do all you can do. Pour yourself into your dream and soon enough it will be ready, lemons and all!

A Line In the Sand

I know that it can be hard to really give your all to something that is either unknown or looks hard. I mean to actually sit down and do work, when it doesn't involve a school assignment? Really?

But believe me when I say, it's so worth it to push yourself and make that commitment. Even though you really get the temptation to get on your phone or computer, just know if you draw that line in the sand and say "I'm doing this no matter what," you'll be one day closer to getting those big monthly checks (or whatever other payday you are looking to have).

Just try not to think of it as work. Think of it this way... the sooner you get it done, the faster it'll all come together and happen for you.

Oh and one more thing in addition to drawing a line in the sand. Remember when I suggested that you use your imagination every day and see your dreams come true in advance? Well, this goes for every night too!

When you close your eyes, imagine what it will feel like when you have all the money you want. And then in the morning, make it a practice to be grateful for at least five things. That's the best way to begin your day. Balance it out.

Visualize your success before you go to bed, and wake up in gratitude for it coming your way each and every day. You don't need to be embarrassed about doing this, or get all self-conscious and freeze up, because really no one but you even has to know... just do it.

End of Chapter Recap:

As a recap to several of the concepts we covered in this chapter, answer to the following questions...

- ✔ What does a "bucket filler" mean to you?
- ✔ List three ways you can be a bucket filler today.
- ✔ What does true success mean to you?
- ✔ List three things you have succeeded at.

BONUS POINTS: Remember, if you have failed in the past, that's a good thing. We often learn more from our failures than from our successes. So take out a piece of paper and write the story of a time you tried something and failed. Maybe it was the first time you tried to ride a bike or swim or you tried out for a team and didn't make it? Write out the failure in a brief story. Now, turn the piece of paper over and write what you learned from your failure, and how it has helped you learn and grow as a person.

Take a little (or big) action step TODAY towards your dream! Go do it now, I believe in you!

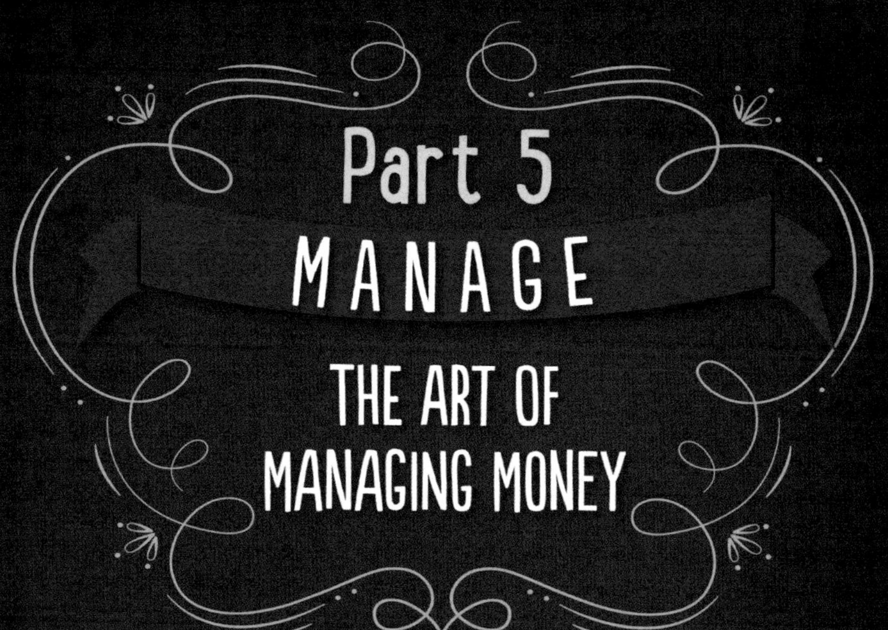

Part 5
MANAGE
THE ART OF MANAGING MONEY

"Once upon a time there was a Miser who used to hide his gold at the foot of a tree in his garden; but every week he used to go and dig it up and gloat over his gains. A robber, who had noticed this, went and dug up the gold and decamped with it. When the Miser next came to gloat over his treasures, he found nothing but the empty hole. He tore his hair, and raised such an outcry that all the neighbors came around him, and he told them how he used to come and visit his gold. 'Did you ever take any of it out?' asked one of them. 'Nay,' said he, 'I only came to look at it.' 'Then come again and look at the hole,' said a neighbor; 'it will do you just as much good.'"

– The Miser and His Gold

THE ART OF MANAGING MONEY

In This Chapter

- ✔ Looking at organization, operations, and branching out
- ✔ Seeing the possibilities of doing more with less personal effort
- ✔ Exploring the world of spending, saving, and giving it away

"MONEY – I'D SAY IT'S BEEN MY BIGGEST PROBLEM ALL MY LIFE. IT TAKES A LOT OF IT TO MAKE DREAMS COME TRUE."

– WALT DISNEY

Aesop's fable "The Miser and His Gold" illustrates the notion of "what good is having money if you don't intend to use it?" Even though saving money for the future is wise, you don't want to become such a miser that you never enjoy the fruits of your labor. If you aren't enjoying money, what's the point of working so hard to get it? There is a fine line to walk between saving and hoarding. The lesson learned is to do your best to not to end up being a miser with your gold.

In this chapter, we will explore how to best manage your money by diving deep into the land of operations and other behind-the-scenes stuff, like paying attention to the details. We'll also take a look at how to expand and multiply our efforts to increase profits. Then we jump into the areas of creating our own financial budgets for success, and cover the aspects of saving, and spending plans. Last but not least, we will take a look at how by using the power of giving and tithing, we can actually accelerate our road to riches.

DELIVER A MONEY PLAN

As your ideas expand and the money begins to come in, you will want to make sure to keep your cash in a safe place. No, not under your mattress, and definitely not by keeping more than a couple hundred bucks in a piggy bank. I would advise you talk to your parents on this one, so they can help you open a student savings account in your name at a bank or financial institution. This way you can carry around a debit card of your own, and at least have your money in a safe place.

I love having my own bank account, debit card, and the freedom of being in control of my own money. Yes, I'm talking about the money I've earned with my own hard work. Let me tell you, it's super cool, and you're going to love it too!

So what to do with the money once you've earned it? Well let's sharpen your money management skills and start thinking about percentages to budget your money around. One suggestion is to keep some of it in reserve to pay for the cost of future sales or making more inventory. That amount will be entirely up to you and your best judgment in determining what percentage to keep on hand to grow your operations.

spending
Tithing
Saving

Some people keep 50%, others use 25% as a guide. Basically just do what feels right for you and your business or project. It's a great idea to find an adult who runs their own business (and is good with money) to help teach you. Or, you might even get an advisor at your local bank who can support and guide you.

Once you have set your future operations reserve aside, I'd recommend you split up the rest of your earning profits similar to the way I do as shown here:

- ✔ Spending = 80%
- ✔ Tithing = 10%
- ✔ Saving = 10%

Spending, tithing and saving. Those are my three main areas of focus. But we get into that more a little later on within this chapter. First, let's take a look at how to organize and keep track of what you are earning.

TIDBIT: If you don't pay attention to the details, your money and profits might feel all lonely, and then just run away from you or get lost. Hey, I'm being serious. You wouldn't want that to happen now would you? lol

DETAILS, DETAILS, DETAILS

Tracking Your Progress

"TWO PEOPLE CAN LOOK AT THE SAME THING
AND SEE IT DIFFERENTLY."
– JUSTIN BIEBER

There are people who are more detail oriented than others, and for some even, it's a real pain in the neck. But if you are like me, it's actually fun tracking your progress and seeing everything neat and organized.

Staying on top of the details can be a breeze. The trick is to create a system to balance and measure everything that works for you and make sure to keep track of everything business related. It can be fun, and if you do this you'll thank me later, really!

In other words, you'll need to balance the books. Even if it's not your thing, you'll need to do this. If you can't or don't want to spend the time doing this, make sure you have a support partner you can count on to do this for you. Bottom line... it is very important.

A System of Records

Having to keep track of inventory (both the materials you need for your products and the finished goods) sales, customers, leads... all of the things related to your business, can seem overwhelming. Especially if don't keep good records or have a system to organize. Here are the main detail areas to pay attention to:

- ✔ prospects, leads, and customers
- ✔ sales
- ✔ inventory
- ✔ expenses
- ✔ profits

And here are the things I do, or things I use (or have someone else do for me) to stay on top of it all:

- ✔ Excel spreadsheets to track sales and expenses
- ✔ Quicken software
- ✔ Cash box
- ✔ Financial report templates

There are many apps out there that can be used to stay organized. And, since I make lots of lists, I found that Notability (a note-taking app for iPad, iPhone and iPod touch) works great for me. I also have a booklet where I write down the money I make or loan out, etc.

The bottom line here is to rely on the philosophy of "build your house on a rock solid foundation instead of sand." Your business is only going to go so far, if you don't keep track of what you are doing.

One example of this is when I helped my Grandma organize around her house. Being that this is such a simple way to make extra money, there's really not very much to keep track of. Mostly, I would bring my smart phone and use the timer to track how much time I actually worked. I then I'd write that down along the way. I'd stop the timer when I'm on a snack break, and then at the end of the day, I would add up the total time worked.

Here's how to do the math. You multiply your hours worked times the hourly rate you're getting paid, and "viola," you get your total amount earned for the time you put in that day.

But, if I didn't track it? I might forget what time I arrived, or how long I was on break, and then it's really not professional at all to guess how much time I actually worked. Whether you are a young adult or teen, you want to present yourself as professionally as possible. Even on simple tasks or chores for pay.

Here's another way to illustrate this. Let's assume you start a neighborhood dog-walking business. You might create an Excel spreadsheet with the addresses (and names if you have them) for all the people who live on your street.

Then, when you go to each house and knock on the door with your flyer or business card, you can track:

- ✔ who you talked to
- ✔ who seems interested so you can follow up next week
- ✔ who said no, they aren't interested
- ✔ who said yes, you're hired!

If you don't keep track as you go, you're bound to forget details of each conversation after visiting six or seven homes. It would be great to also write down if they have a dog or not, the kind of dog, size, and breed etc...so when you do go back and talk to the owner again, they feel like you paid attention and care about them.

TIP: If you visit www.MyMomIsNotMyMoney.com you will find some very helpful resources already designed and created to help you with tracking your business.

Follow-Through

The next thing you should make sure to have, is a great system of follow-through. That means following up with both your customers and with your future customers (and also with your suppliers and partners). Make sure you use a tracking system for contact management that includes things like:

- ✔ name, address, phone, and email
- ✔ what they purchased and when
- ✔ interests or hobbies
- ✔ notes on what contact you have had to date

The better your records are kept, the better you will be able to serve your customer's needs. It's that personal touch, and sometimes going that extra mile, that'll be the difference between just having customers, and having raving fans loving everything you have and you do.

For example, if you are in the business of selling cupcakes door to door, you can track which homes purchased your cupcakes and which ones didn't, just by writing that down on a notepad (or a sales tracking sheet) while you are out selling.

And then when you get back home, you can create a simple follow-up card with a coupon for 10% off their next purchase, as well as a thank you to give your customers to let them know you appreciate their business.

People really do love thank you notes, and the coupon is also a fun idea to help create your next sale and keep them as happy (and repeat) customers.

MANAGING THE CLOCK

Time-Sucking "Vampires"

"TIME EXPANDS TO MEET MY EVERY NEED."
– AUTHOR UNKNOWN

One of the biggest issues for most people is, "I don't have enough time." Well, unless something has changed, everyone I know has the same amount... a full 24 hours each and every day, right?

So why do some people get more accomplished than others? I say it comes down to time management. You are either good at it, or you are not. Well maybe there are points in-between, but you get the idea.

Case in point, kids who have the same classes as me seem to spend hours doing their homework at home, even on the weekends. Honestly, I usually don't have very much homework. That's because I tend to get it done in class or in the extra minutes waiting for my parents to pick me up and driving home. Most kids are using that time to relax and goof off instead.

The trick is to manage your time well so you can do all the things you really want to do (while still getting enough sleep too). Take a look at trying out some of these ideas to find what works best for you.

Gadgets and Social Media

We all know that in today's world, there seem to be a lot of time stealers. In other words, gadgets, TV, video games, instant chat with friends, etc. etc. on and on... I'm pretty sure you get the idea here and know where I'm going with this!

Check in for yourself. How many of these activities do you spend time (even hours) with each day?

- ✔ TV shows
- ✔ Facebook, Twitter, and Instagram
- ✔ Cell phones
- ✔ Facetime
- ✔ Mobile apps and games
- ✔ Text messaging

We are so used to having a device by our side, we sometimes let these gadgets consume our lives. Ha! Right now I'm seeing this picture in my mind of us as robots relying on gadgets to get us through the day.

So let me ask you this: when was the last time you spent a day with your family without constantly checking your notifications and texts? Whenever I go to a restaurant, I almost always see these little kids playing on their iPads or iPhones and not talking to their parents. Or I see the parents texting and not noticing their kids. What's that all about?!

This is crazy when you really look at it. I'm not saying I don't use technology. Of course I do... I live in the 21st century, right? But wouldn't it be nice for a change to leave our gadgets and devices in our rooms and come down to be with the family, to connect with them and not just the brightness of little screen?

Well maybe not, if your little brother who annoys you is there too, but you know what I mean, right? (I was just kidding bro...I still love you!)

PRODUCTIVITY TIP: Get what you need to get done first so you have more free time before dinner, etc. Do not procrastinate! Or it might just bite you in the butt.

Expanding Time and Space

For example, do an experiment and keep track of the time you spend on your activities throughout the day. There are some really cool time tracking apps to use. My favorite is www.toggl.com, which tracks every second of every hour... then creates reports and graphs of how you are spending your time.

Here's a test. For one whole week, track how much time you are at school, doing homework, talking on the phone, using your iPad or computer, on Instagram, etc. Keep track of every minute each day for a week. Then have Toggl add it up show you the results.

You may be surprised at how much time is really consumed once you see these little blocks of time all added up. On average, kids 8-18 years old spend nearly 44.5 hours per week online. That's more than the average adult spends at work! It's one thing to search the web to learn things, but be careful if you're just spending time on games and stuff like that. Keep asking yourself, is this going to help me grow and move forward? Then try and cut down the time you spend doing things that won't matter in a few months.

DUPLICATE YOUR EFFORTS

Looking back at history you will see that most of the really, really rich people had this in common. They made their money work for them and had multiple streams of income that made money while they slept.

How cool would that be to have money made on your behalf even while you were sleeping? Well, it worked for these successful people back in the day, and it certainly still works now. Besides, there is no "closed" sign hanging on the Internet last time I checked.

MAKING MONEY IN YOUR SLEEP

Expanding Your Business

"THERE ARE THOSE WHO LOOK AT THINGS THE WAY THEY ARE, AND ASK WHY... I DREAM OF THINGS THAT NEVER WERE, AND ASK WHY NOT?"

– ROBERT KENNEDY

So how does this apply to you? Well, why not sell an e-book online? Think of something you know how to do, and turn it into a book. Maybe you think what you know is no big deal, but others might think it is a big deal and want to learn about it. So you can write a "How-To" guide about something you are good at and sell it on Amazon. Really, this works. I know a kid who made thousands of dollars by selling an e-book about how to skate-board! That's crazy, right?

What if you know some cool baby-sitting tips, or how to create fun and unique hair styles, or if you know how to knit, or build your own video games? All these things, and way more, are of interest to other people who would be willing to pay money to learn how to do these things. That could be from you (or someone else who is also enterprising... like you) that is selling a "how-to guide" online and is earning money from it.

For more "how-to" e-book ideas go to my website (the URL is in the back of this book if you've forgotten). There you will find that I've researched and share some great ideas for you.

Even if you have a simple idea and are just getting started on your journey to riches, there's no reason to not begin thinking about how you might expand your business. If not now, at least somewhere down the road (or in the near future). By adding more elements and layers to what you offer for sale, or by bringing in a partner and expanding with new ideas, there are many ways to improve and amplify your initial business ideas into something bigger and better.

Multiplying Your Efforts

Expand

Duplicate

And how about branching out and duplicating your efforts by franchising? Think Subway or McDonald's. Once you have a good idea and find that people like what it is that you have, begin to think about ways you might package what you do and offer to teach others to do the same. You never know, you might just have the next best franchiseable idea. And once that becomes a reality, you can start counting dollars in your sleep, rather than sheep.

Not only can you expand and duplicate your business ideas and efforts, but you can also branch out into additional add-on or sequel types of activities. Think of it like a great movie trilogy such as Transformers or Superman or Indiana Jones. People liked the first movie so well, that they kept coming up with sequels that were similar to the original, but different and improved perhaps (or sometimes not... lol).

But seriously, when you come up with something that people like, begin to think of ways to improve on or duplicate that success. Like for example, you have a really successful lemonade stand business. Couldn't that be expanded into being a fruit and vegetable stand too? Then perhaps, you expand into adding nuts and organic dried fruits and candies. Get the idea?

MARKETING PARTNERSHIPS

Enlisting the Experts

"I BELIEVE THAT BEING SUCCESSFUL MEANS HAVING A BALANCE OF SUCCESS STORIES ACROSS THE MANY AREAS OF YOUR LIFE."
– ZIG ZIGLAR

This can work really well by partnering up with others who are doing something similar to you. Instead of becoming the expert in everything, find people around you who are experts in something that complements what you are doing. For example, you sell a line of custom jewelry, and you have a friend who makes decorated jeweled denim clothing. Do you see how these are a perfect match to sell together? One line complements the other, and you have a chance to expand your business by selling to their customers as well as your own (and vice versa). How cool is that?

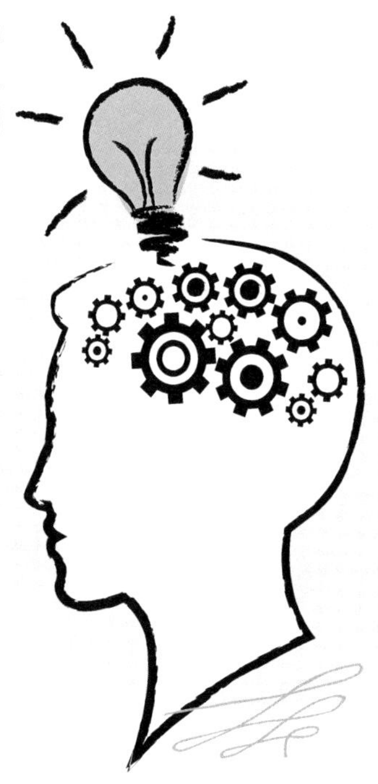

Here are some other ideas that can work well together:

- ✔ A tutor and a babysitter
- ✔ A dog walker and pet sitter
- ✔ Mowing lawns and raking leaves

Just try and brainstorm on things that complement and work well together. That way your marketing and sales efforts can be combined for greater impact. In other words, you can give them a one-two punch for the same effort behind just one activity.

Investing in Others

Another thing you can do to branch out and expand your business efforts is to think about investing in another person's business ideas. And it doesn't always take money to invest, sometimes you can lend a hand or a talent and work into an ownership position by what they call "sweat-equity" (which means you work for your position). All of this might be down the road for you because you are just getting started making money for yourself, but don't count it out or say it's out of the question at your age. Nothing is impossible unless you believe it is. Right?

For example, let's say my neighbor wants to start a duct-tape business making wallets, bracelets, bows, key chains, etc. and my brother would like to get involved... but he does not really want to have his own business. He would invest his "sweat-equity" (using his skills and time, but not his money) to help make the products and then share a percentage of the profits.

DIVVY UP THE PIE

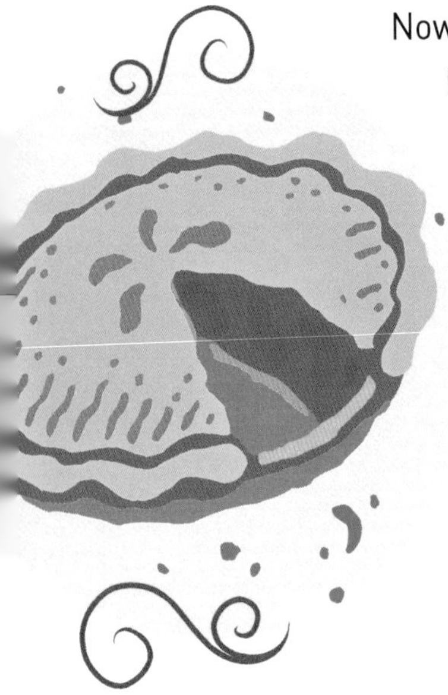

Now we are getting to what for me is the really fun part. Splitting up the "money" pie. I love seeing how much money I can keep and how much I can save for later, but I also love seeing that by my efforts, I help make someone's life a little bit better.

CASE IN POINT: I began this book project with the idea of giving a $100,000.00 donation check to charity as my 10% tithe. My thought is I'd like to help support St. Jude's Hospital who in turn supports families going through the cancer treatment process. I read a book last year

A Fault In Our Stars that really got me passionate about helping people with cancer.

So I now have a deeper reason to give. Part of my book-writing endeavors means I also keep visualizing that $100k check being presented to St. Jude's Hospital.

SPENDING WISELY

Disciplined Budgets

"DREAMS CAN BECOME A REALITY WHEN WE POSSESS A VISION THAT IS CHARACTERIZED BY THE WILLINGNESS TO WORK HARD, A DESIRE FOR EXCELLENCE, AND A BELIEF IN OUR RIGHT AND OUR RESPONSIBILITY TO BE EQUAL MEMBERS OF SOCIETY."
– JANET JACKSON

So, let's get back to the managing details part and focus on those things that will help our business ideas to become really successful. That way we will have more money to spend, save, and give away, right?

Chunks to Yourself

Remember back to when I said that after you tuck away your operations reserve "kitty", then with what is left you could split up the rest like I do with the 80/10/10 rule? Well let's dive into that again here.

The "spending 80%" portion will be the money spent on clothes, games, gadgets, and basically anything else you want to buy with your own money (and NOT your mom's – how fun is that?!).

As I said, I suggest you keep 80% of your earnings for that fun stuff, tithe or give away another 10%, and save the remaining 10%. But remember this is after you set aside money for your future operational needs.

For example, I know of one kid who actually puts the 80% back into his operating fund because he wants to build a really, really big business someday and doesn't want to have to ask others to invest in his business if he can do it on his own. You decide here what's best for you.

Chunks to Save

The "saving 10%" is the next thing. This is the money you set aside for future things. A phone, car, college, or a house. I know it can be hard to put money aside, but you'll be glad later when you have it. By splitting these amounts up in the beginning, it doesn't let you spend all of the money right then and there, just on yourself. And, pretty soon, you will have more in your savings account than you realize.

Especially if you are one of those who ends up with a different % split and puts more into a savings account instead of a spending account. These people often are saving up for something big, and want to get it sooner instead of later. So, since everyone has their own comfort levels, I just recommend that you set some rules in the beginning and be disciplined to follow them, so you have a solid budget structure.

Impulse and Instant Gratification

Of course, don't be impulsive and spend everything on yourself. I encourage you to be smart while spending. And don't recommend getting into the habit of buying random, ridiculous things because you want a lifetime supply of it. Or 'cuz it's on sale.

Just because the price is right, doesn't necessarily mean the item is right for you. Only buy something if the item is a complete "10" on your rating scale. Really, it's got to be a perfect 10!

Here's a great tip on how to know if you should buy something, or not. Once, about three years ago, I went shopping at Abercrombie and spent $200.00 for no real reason. I spent all that money on just an impulse because I liked what was on display in the store.

I ended up regretting it and felt like I had actually lost all of that money. Ever since then, I switch it up and think instead, "Will I regret leaving without this item?" Or I ask, "How will I feel a week from now with or without this item? Is it really a 10, or even a 12?"

10 Second Rule

Sometimes just putting something on hold and going out to look at the other stores will do the trick. If you can't stop thinking about that item, then return to that store and get it. Remember, you are the one who put in the effort to get your money, so you deserve to spend it as you want.

That item may, or may not, be something you really want and will use for a long time. So, you should always set a budget for yourself. Don't just take $300.00 in your wallet to go shopping if your budget is only $180.00. Deal with your money wisely. And if for some reason you end up making a mistake, don't worry too much. The only way to learn is to move on and get over your obstacles. And do better next time.

PAY IT FORWARD

The Power of Giving

"I absolutely believe in the power of tithing and giving back. My own experience about all the blessings I've had in my life is that the more I give away, the more that comes back. That is the way life works, and that is the way energy works."
– Ken Blanchard

Did you ever see the movie "Pay It Forward?" That was such an inspiring movie to watch. The story is about this 12-year-old kid whose social studies teacher gives an assignment to "think of something to change the world and put it into action."

The kid comes up with the idea of paying a favor not back, but forward by doing new good deeds for three new people. And his idea becomes a revolution, in a good way. This just goes to show how even the small things can make a big difference. I love the idea of paying it forward, and giving money to great causes.

By following the simple principle of tithing, it puts more meaning into what I am doing... knowing that some extra good is coming from it and not just for me.

What's Tithing?

What is this tithing thing I've been talking about anyway? I know, maybe you've never even heard of tithing before, or you may only have some experience with it from church or other non-profit organizations.

Basically, tithing is the art of giving away some of your earnings right off the top. You can choose any number of great causes to contribute to, or you can simply give it away to someone or something that has made a positive difference in your life.

Like an inspiring author or minister, and not just your church. Wherever, or whatever you end up choosing to contribute to, the practice is to give away part of what you get, and to keep the flow of money circulating and doing good in a variety and multitude of ways.

Ten percent is a good amount to work with for tithing. It is always good to give money out to others and for good causes, because first, it supports people in need, and also whatever you give out, you end up receiving more coming back to you.

It just happens that way. Kinda like gravity, somehow tithing expands the good that keeps coming your way.

Also, you can feel great about buying this book (or whoever bought it for you can) because 10% of the purchase is being sent to St. Jude's. As I said before, I'm giving away 10% of all the proceeds received for this book to St. Jude's Hospital to support kids with cancer. This feels right to me, and both you and I can feel good about how this tithing can really help these kids and their families through a difficult time.

Again, I'd suggest you give 10% like I am, because it seems fair, not too little, but just enough. Some people like to tithe even more, so do whatever feels good for you. But there is research that shows, people who are givers are often more successful. Think about that.

A Triple Crown Win

This is where everyone wins. And I believe it's the very best way to do any business venture. To have a win-win-win scenario, is when the seller, the buyer, and everyone around you wins. Just like in the "Pay It Forward" example... it becomes a revolution.

Here's an example of a win-win-win:

- ✔ I write the *My Mom Is Not My Money* book and earn money for a new car, college, etc.
- ✔ I "pay it forward" by teaching you how to be financially successful yourself.
- ✔ I donate 10% to St Jude's hospital...

You see how it's a three-way win? And how about this. By taking it one step further, I can even donate some of my books for free to *Playground*

Of Dreams, an afterschool program supporting underprivileged kids who go after their dreams, making it a quadruple win!

Another example is with Tom's Shoes. For every pair of their shoes sold, a child in a third world country gets a free pair of shoes. When someone buys a pair of shoes, Tom's makes a profit, the buyer gets to take part in doing a good deed for kids in need, and the children in need get a much needed pair of shoes.

You can also take a look at "shopwithmeaning.org" or find many other companies that follow the "buy-one, give-one-away" philosophy. For instance, with Kyle Yamaguchi and Shu-Chu Wu, "141 Eyewear" has a mission of making a difference to those in critical need of prescription eyewear around the globe with a "buy-one, give-one" glasses company. How cool is that?

End of Chapter Recap:

Once again, think of answers to the following questions...

- ✔ What are some of the time-sucking activities I could delete in my day-to-day life?
- ✔ What are some ideas I have that might turn into a "making money in my sleep" activity?
- ✔ What experts can I enlist in my marketing efforts?
- ✔ What are some great causes that I would like to donate a portion of my earnings to?

BONUS POINTS: When I was back in the 5th grade, my class decided to support a group of kids in Africa who didn't have money to go to school otherwise. I decided to take my entire savings and give it to that fund to help these kids, and I felt really good after I did.

I invite you to remember your deeper "WHY," or the reason you are making money (we talked about this in the beginning of this book), and also where you might want to give or donate some of your money... such as to a cause.

Then write down your own "giving" goals and be as specific as you can. As mentioned before, a great way to think of this is 10% of the total income goal that you have.

Example, if your goal is to make $100, then you would plan on giving $10 to a good cause, or your church, or a local food bank. That is a good place to start.

Conclusion

The main point of this book is for you to learn how to support yourself, not rely on other people, and along the way develop a great amount of self-confidence. I hope that you take these lessons and apply them to your life, study them, so you can become financially free and not have to worry about the gas prices rising or paying taxes. Thank you so much for supporting me in buying this book!!! I really appreciate it and hope for you amazing results, incredible income, and most importantly that you develop your character... because at the end of the day, that is what is most important. And always remember...

ME AND MY MC

your mom is most definitely NOT your money!

For more
moneymaking ideas,
action items,
FREE GIFTS, simple forms,
and more, visit:
www.MyMomIsNotMyMoney.com

Made in the USA
Charleston, SC
02 March 2016